# CRAFTING A CONTINUUM

Rethinking

Contemporary

Craft

# CRAFTING A

## Rethinking
## Contemporary
## Craft

Edited by Peter Held
and Heather Sealy Lineberry

Catalogue coordinator, Elizabeth Kozlowski

**AMUSEUM**

# CONTINUUM

This book was published in conjunction with an exhibition organized by the Arizona State University Art Museum and its Ceramics Research Center.

Arizona State University Art Museum
Herberger Institute for Design and the Arts
Tenth Street and Mill Avenue
Tempe, AZ 82587 2911
TEL. 480 965 2787  FAX 480 965 5254
asumuseum.asu.edu

Catalogue produced
for Arizona State University
by Perpetua Press, Santa Barbara, CA
Edited by Tish O'Connor
Designed by Dana Levy
Printed in China by Toppan Printing Co.

ISBN 0-9817957
Distributed by University of North Carolina Press

Library of Congress
Catalogue-in-Publication Data
    *Crafting A Continuum: Rethinking Contemporary Craft*
    Edited by Peter Held and Heather Sealy Lineberry,
    essays by Peter Held, Heather Sealy Lineberry, Jenni Sorkin, Synnøve Vik
        Catalogue of an exhibition of the same name organized by
            Arizona State University Art Museum
        Includes bibliographic references and index
        ISBN: 9781469612805 (hardcover: alk. paper)
    1. Arizona State University Art Museum Collections
    2. Decorative arts—Philosophy
    3. Design—Philosophy
    4. 20th Century Exhibitions
    5. 21st Century Exhibitions
    I. Held, Peter, 1951-, Lineberry, Heather Sealy, 1963-
    II. Arizona State University Art Museum.
    III. Title.

Cover:
Mark Newport
*W Man*, 2009
Hand-knit acrylic, buttons

Back Cover:
Anders Ruhwald
*Form and Function, # 2*, 2006
Glazed earthenware, painted steel, piping, rubber caps

P 1–3
Matthias Pliessnig
*Brace*, 2012
White oak, copper

**ASU** Art Museum
ARIZONA STATE UNIVERSITY

# CONTENTS

# ACKNOWLEDGMENTS

T HIS PUBLICATION COMES AT A PIVOTAL JUNCTURE WHEN THE CRAFT FIELD IN AMERICA, and elsewhere, grapples with an identity crisis that has been percolating over the last two decades. As cultural, socio-economic, technological, and generational shifts reshape our worldview, all aspects of the meaning of craft are open for debate.

The Windgate Charitable Foundation has been a true beacon of light for American craft during this transitional period. Their support of this project provided the necessary funds to fully realize this exhibition and catalogue, new acquisitions, our visiting artist series, and allowed us to assess our collection while adding a new level of scholarship to the field. Our sincere gratitude goes to the Foundation's trustees for their enthusiasm and confidence in the project, and to Robyn and John Horn for their ongoing support.

During the course of this two-year project, the curatorial staff was able to make numerous studio, museum, and gallery visits both in the U.S. and abroad. This research proved invaluable as we sought artists that were innovative makers and thoughtful about future practices and possibilities. These curatorial visits as well as the visiting artists at ASU expanded our knowledge and broadened our approach to collecting in the future. Thank you all who made this project so rewarding.

The two primary essayists for this publication deserve much credit for their incisive and thoughtful observations. Our deepest gratitude goes to Jenni Sorkin for her essay that looks back at past educational craft programs and residencies to assess their impact, and to Synnøve Vik, who investigates globalization and its effect on both culture and craft. Separately and together, they capture a distinct moment in craft history as we grapple with its future. This publication is much richer because of their scholarship and insightful readings of the field.

*Crafting a Continuum* will travel to five museums on its national tour after the exhibition is inaugurated at the Arizona State University Art Museum. We sincerely thank the museums and their staff for enthusiastically embracing the exhibition and attendant educational programs. The tour schedule, listed on page 192, will provide an opportunity for a broad audience to become familiar with the full range of the museum's collection in craft-based media and the current dialogue in the field.

Of equal importance to the presentation of the exhibition is this publication. We are indebted to graphic designer Dana Levy and editor Tish O'Connor of Perpetua Press, Santa Barbara, who produce art books and exhibition catalogues for museums throughout the United States. Generous collaborators, they have been sensitive in showcasing the artists' work to its best advantage. Many thanks as well to all the skilled photographers, listed on page 191, particularly Craig Smith who photographed the majority of our collection.

This exhibition and attendant publication would not have been possible without the institutional support of Arizona State University. We would like to thank Arizona State University president Michael Crow; Dr. Kwang-Wu Kim, former dean and director of the Herberger Institute for Design and the Arts; and Gordon Knox, director of the ASU Art Museum.

Elizabeth Kozlowski, Windgate Charitable Foundation curatorial fellow, provided outstanding research, support, and management from start to finish. Without her steadfastness, diligence, knowledge, and insights, *Crafting a Continuum* would not have been realized in its present form.

Anders Ruhwald, a talented sculptor who was a visiting artist in 2012, articulated a deep understanding of object placement during his lecture. He seemed to be a natural choice when we considered an exhibition designer for the project. His intellectual prowess and wit made for a dynamic installation. Our sincere thanks to Nancy Tieken, a friend of the museum, who made it possible to have Anders be part of our team. Anne Sullivan, registrar, and Elisa Benavidez Hayes, assistant registrar, ably managed the myriad of details with loan forms, packing, and transportation of works. Stephen Johnson, head preparator, and his able design and installation team always put the artists' work in its best light. It is our good fortune to be surrounded by such talented professionals.

This reevaluation of the collection that was built by former and current ASU Art Museum directors and curators has reminded us to be thankful for their dedicated commitment and passion and for the support of the students, faculty, generous collectors and museum supporters, and artists who contributed to their work and ours. Our hope is that a growing audience will come to appreciate their many contributions to the craft field over the last five decades and will help lead us well into the future.

# INTRODUCTION

CRAFTING A CONTINUUM:

WHAT IS ENDURING IN CRAFT? WHAT IS ITS FUTURE?

Continuity and craft run deep and long and tie each of us to all of us. Craft is directly and intimately linked to the making process: the Old English craeft and Old Norse kraptr meant strength, skill, and virtue, particularly in making. The hand and intention of the maker are embedded in the craft object, and so the creation and release of that object forges a connection between maker and user (or viewer). Because we are all part of the warp and weft of community, where that craft object dwells in the world and how it connects to others and to society also become defining qualities of craft. Craft is suspended in, and part of, the community from which it emerges. Craft is a handmade object connected to its cultural context and to the community through its use or purpose, including less tangible contributions such as the ability to convey ideas, to document a story, record history, declare identity, or communicate affect and meaning. The continuum of craft starts with the first actions of humans—the collecting, preparing, and sharing of food, drink, cloths, story, home, hearth, and history.

The maker, the object, and its cultural context are three core elements of craft; meaning that emerges through the interaction and overlapping of these three elements explains that imprecise yet undeniable emotional response that a craft object can trigger. As far forward as we can see, objects and object making connected to our collective humanness will always carry deep import and speak richly to us.

A core element in any definition of art includes the thoughtful, focused exploration of the world: what we know or feel, the identification of patterns, how systems work, and a critical, alert, exploratory way of knowing the world. Another essential aspect of any understanding of art includes that profound humanitarian gesture of attempting to move an understanding or idea from one heart or head to another; this is the dialogue, the relationship between the artist (the maker), and the audience (the user).

For the viewer, art is that conversation, that movement of ideas, between the art object (be it a painting, a play, or music) and themselves. For the artist, art is an active process combining research, effort, and a disciplined exploration of some aspect of the world - it entails following an idea, assembling an insight and allowing that to emerge into communicable form. Ideally, the art experience is an active, dialogue-based process engaging both artist and viewer; an emotional and intellectual process enriched with uncertainty and ambiguity, both necessary elements of any complex contemplation.

Like language, art and craft are embedded in community. Craft is tied to community by being linked to the object and the making process in a more direct way than the so-called fine arts must be. The conceptual arts of the past century took the idea or concept as the most important part of an artwork and framed the making of the object as a simple mechanical secondary phase. De-emphasizing the role of making and arguing that an idea itself can be the art object increased the separation between craft and art. The primacy of the idea over the making may still differentiate craft from art, but the connection and similarity of craft and art runs deeper and further back—to their common relationship with society and the expression and exploration of ideas and aesthetics.

Sonya Clark
*Threadwrapped in Blue and Brown*, 2008 (detail)
Combs, thread

It is in their relationship to society that arts and crafts meet and intertwine. If in the twentieth century the fine arts took a heady conceptual turn, moving ultimately to accept the disembodied concept as art-object, then in the twenty-first century we foresee the arts returning to a more vital—actualized—relationship with society. The art have been finding their way back to the common ground they share with crafts; both art and craft dwell in the community, are understood to be part of it, and are implemental in its evolution. Socially engaged art practice, which moves out of the white cube of exhibition space and relocates contemporary art discourse to the actual world in which actual people live, is a prime example of art returning to the space it shares with craft. Often today artists approach this discourse directly through interventions, installations, actions, and social engagement and by developing their research from within the fabric of an active social world. Going to society itself to explore an idea or present a critique confirms and revalues the collective. Contemporary art practices now rub shoulders with crafts; the collective is the locus of craft and the craft object displays a clear relationship to the community that they are built in and for.

Both craft and art emerge from and operate in the same territory—the living, morphing, and transforming collective that is us. Craft fits perfectly in any art museum or collection that encompasses the contemporary.

The mission for museums today—and one goal of educational institutions everywhere—is to impart an understanding that we are suspended in a shared, collectively constructed web of meaning and knowledge, a collaborative reality that is ever changing and always expanding. This cumulative pool of knowledge is the basis of reality.

Crafts come from within the community and exist for it: their presence references our collective nature. Like all the arts, crafts are here to stay, both as a celebration of making—that encompasses both materials and maker—and as a physical manifestation of the collective nature of our species. Our ability to change and grow our shared reality depends on our ability to recognize that we truly are all in this together and that we are adding to it (making it up) as we go along.

I would like to thank the Windgate Charitable Foundation for the unswerving support it has provided the ASU Art Museum in the past and for its invaluable encouragement that helped us realize this exhibition, catalogue, and related programming. The museum is a fuller and more complete institution because of the Foundation's inspired investment.

GORDON KNOX, director

Arizona State University Art Museum

Closing reception, *Jarbas Lopes: Cicloviaéra*, Arizona State University Art Museum, 2007

# PREFACE

Peter Held

Heather Sealy Lineberry

Rudy Turk stands by Robert Arneson's *Flat Face*, 1981, part of *Director's Choice*, the last exhibition he curated prior to retirement. Turk became aware of Arneson's work while he directed the Richmond Art Center in northern California from 1960 to 1965.

Exterior view, Arizona State University Art Museum

THE ARIZONA STATE UNIVERSITY ART MUSEUM HAS AN EXTENSIVE HISTORY OF INFLUENTIAL collecting and presenting of contemporary craft with a media emphasis on ceramics, fiber and baskets, and turned wood. The foundation for these collections was laid by Rudy Turk during his twenty-five-year tenure (1967–1992) as director of the Arizona State University Art Museum. His prescient vision has resulted in one of the more extensive holdings of post–World War II craft in the United States. Its strength lies in its depth, diversity, and quality.

When Turk came to the museum as its new director, the collection he inherited had little more than one hundred historic American and Mexican paintings. Lured here by the university administration's ambitious promise of a new museum building within three years (it eventually took twenty-two), he quickly learned to channel his youthful exuberance into making the most of a shoestring budget and makeshift exhibition spaces. Through a practiced combination of persistence and cajolery, he multiplied the museum's holdings many times over.

Beginning in the 1970s, the Museum was one of a few fine arts institutions to consciously undertake building a studio collection. Craft-based media was relegated in most institutions to a minor form as a decorative or applied art, an explicit instance of the art-versus-craft debate that would rage throughout the next decades. Historically, museums departmentalized media and had specialist curators oversee their holdings, more so in larger institutions. Cross-pollination was scant in both museums and academic programs and, with a few notable exceptions, art hierarchies were rigid throughout the modernist period. In the burgeoning craft world, media-specific organizations, collector circles, artist collectives, commercial galleries, and fairs began to build critical recognition for contemporary craft. While this progression helped craft gain momentum and prestige in the last half of the twentieth century, theories of postmodernism, changing curricula at the university level, and a fluctuating commodity and technological culture have brought about its current reassessment.

Turk valued the craft object as both artifact and, contrary to prevailing biases, art. His maverick approach to curating was rooted in a steadfast refusal to segregate art forms based solely on media. Such traditional museum and art-world hierarchies, he felt, created artificial boundaries between objects, practice, and ideas. His penchant for collecting broadly set the tone for an art museum infused with an interdisciplinary vigor and an embrace of new art forms and ideas. His final contribution to this institution was guiding the process of creating the ASU Art Museum's architectural gem, the Nelson Fine Arts Center, which was designed by Antoine Predock in 1989.

At a university museum, the curators strive to be agents of change and engagement, and to create a meeting point of ideas through our exhibitions, projects, community programs, and academic research. Closely allied with all academic units that encompass the Herberger Institute for Design and the Arts, we believe that designers, artists, architects, performers, and creative scholars are essential to our world today. Creativity not only enhances our culture, it broadens our vision, deepens our understanding, and enables us to innovate, grow, and change.

## FIBER AND BASKETS

In 1990 the ASU Art Museum cosponsored the exhibition, *Meeting Ground: Basketry Traditions and Sculptural Forms*, curated by Margo Shermeta, an early theorist and curator of contemporary baskets.[1] The exhibition strove to "provide a break in the line of contemporary basket exhibitions"[2] and studied the new possibilities in the developing connections between traditional baskets and sculptural forms. The thirteen selected artists,[3] many of whom are now represented in the museum collection, shared interests in traditional hand processes and natural materials, yet the work explored a range of concepts in addition to function. *Meeting Ground* established the museum's philosophy of understanding and presenting baskets within the broader context of contemporary sculpture.

*Intertwined: Contemporary Baskets from the Sara and David Lieberman Collection* further marked the museum's commitment to innovations with the basket form. Curated in 2006 by Heather Sealy Lineberry and artist/gallerist Jane Sauer, the exhibition offered a broad overview of the fascinating blend of ancient and contemporary that is characteristic of basketry and charted the range of approaches in contemporary basket making. All of the artists in the exhibition drew upon historic techniques, materials, or forms but tweaked these traditions with innovations that reflected their time and their lives. *Intertwined* traveled to five different venues from coast to coast for two years, and was the occasion for presenting regional and national symposia at several points on its tour.[4]

Installation view, *Intertwined: Contemporary Baskets from the Sara and David Lieberman Collection*, 2005

While its contemporary fiber collection is significantly smaller than its holdings in ceramics and wood, the ASU Art Museum has already played a significant role in the development of the field of contemporary baskets through these seminal exhibitions. The museum's collection reflects these influential exhibitions, with many of the same artists represented by works that both reference tradition and explore innovative new approaches.

Installation view, *Moulthrop Generations: Turned Wood Bowls by Ed, Philip, and Matt Moulthrop*, 2007

## TURNED WOOD

In 1990 Phoenix collector, arts supporter, and attorney Edward "Bud" Jacobson generously gifted his collection of more than ninety turned-wood bowls by contemporary American artists to the ASU Art Museum. Jacobson consciously set out to build the first comprehensive collection of turned wood, inspired by the conviction that "works of the contemporary master turners deserve to be seen by the art—in addition to the craft—audience."[5] After discovering an Ed Moulthrop tiger-striped Georgia pine bowl at The Hand and The Spirit Gallery in Scottsdale in 1977, Jacobson talked with gallerists and artists and systematically built his watershed collection, gathering works by all of the major artists at a time when the field was moving from the functional to the sculptural.

The Jacobson collection documents trends from the 1970s through the 1980s—the growing diversity of technique and materials; vessel and sculptural forms (with an emphasis on the former); a focus on the natural beauty of wood; and early innovations in shape and surface design. The collection covers a vast range of approaches, from delicate paper-thin madrona wood bowls and goblets by Del Stubbs to the massive, ragged rim works of Mark Lindquist; and includes both emerging artists at the time like Arizona-based Todd Hoyer and such national figures as Bob Stocksdale.

Edward "Bud" Jacobson gifted the Jacobson Collection of Turned-Wood Bowls to the Arizona State University Art Museum

The original collection was exhibited at the ASU Art Museum, the Renwick Gallery of the Smithsonian Institution, and twelve national venues from 1985 to 1989. The exhibition tour and book elicited enthusiastic audiences and reviews, including a surprised and admiring article by Roberta Smith in *The New York Times* that brought broad recognition of turned-wood objects as art rather than utilitarian objects. The Jacobson collection had identified an emerging field of professional artists: that important role continues to be cited in its influence on a whole generation of artists and collectors that established turned wood as an art form.

Installation view, Ceramics Research Center's open storage. Foreground: Robert Arneson, *Ground Zero*, 1983

The presence of the Jacobson collection at ASU has substantially influenced the museum's collecting and exhibiting of contemporary art in wood. Beginning in the early 1990s the museum mounted a series of juried exhibitions called *Redefining the Lathe Turned Object* that focused on further developments in turning and younger and emerging artists. The exhibitions were accompanied by national symposia that brought artists, collectors, and curators together for hands-on workshops, scholarly presentations, critiques, and conversations. The final exhibition in the series, *Turned Wood Now, 1997–1998*, was curated by art critic and scholar John Perreault and included ten mid-career turners who were making significant contributions to an established field. Since that time, primarily with support from the Windgate Charitable Foundation and Robyn and John Horn, the museum has extended the collection thoughtfully to cover developments in the field: adding works created on and off the lathe; by artists working in wood from craft and sculpture traditions; and increasing the number of women artists working with wood.

## CERAMICS

Installation view, *Dulce: Bisque Without Borders*, 2011 by Franco Mondini-Ruiz

The collection of 315 contemporary works by 120 British and American ceramists that Anne and Sam Davis gifted to ASU Art Museum in 1998 raised the profile of the collection and captured the attention of ceramic collectors nationwide. With additional gifts made on the establishment in 2002 of the Ceramics Research Center (CRC), the collection now numbers close to 4,000 objects. It is dominated by American ceramic artists and, to a large extent, by functional or vessel-oriented objects. In recent years, the scope of the collection has been broadened to become more international and includes British studio ceramics primarily from the 1980s, works by artists who are allied as CoBrA (an acronym formed from abbreviations of the cities in which they worked, Copenhagen, Brussels, and Amsterdam), and more diverse representation of emerging and established artists from Asia and Europe.

Since its inception the collection has embraced representative works by artists that reflect the social, cultural, and historical activities of the world. As a study collection for students and researchers, the holdings demonstrate the full range of techniques, aesthetic approaches, and possibilities within the medium. This panoramic survey provides a genealogy of American ceramics in the last six decades. While several prominent artist-educators are represented in depth—Robert Arneson, Rudy Autio, Warren MacKenzie, Patti Warashina, and Betty Woodman, to name a few—so too are several generations of their students. This visual pedigree provides both evidence of the teacher's impact on the field as well as the artistic influences that have marked the latter part of the twentieth century.

Rudy Turk was emphatic about keeping the collections accessible, a goal that was largely accomplished with open storage. At any given time, approximately 20 percent of the collection is on view in clear storage cases. As a university museum, service to the student population is imperative. The School of Art, with one of the leading undergraduate and graduate ceramics programs led by three full-time faculty, benefits from having the use of the collection. The display of objects, which is periodically reinstalled to provide an ever-changing perspective on the collection, offers a glimpse of the breadth and scope of ASU's holdings.

The scholar and artist Susan Peterson was already active with the university when early in the new century she began discussing it as the repository for the archives she had created in researching Shoji Hamada, Lucy Lewis, and Maria Martinez—the subject of three of her books—and many technical and aesthetic aspects of ceramics. Her files, films, books, and slides from a career of research and publishing form the centerpiece of the center's archives, shifting its emphasis from simply amassing work to the active study of ceramics and dissemination of research through exhibitions, publications, and programs. The establishment of the CRC in a university setting addressed the need for increased scholarship and substantive exhibitions in the field, and made our collection central to that mission.

An initiative of solo retrospective and mid-career exhibitions of major innovators in ceramics commenced in 2005. The profiled artists have included Wayne Higby, Karen Karnes, David Shaner, Akio Takamori, and ASU Regents professor Kurt Weiser. We hoped that recognizing these creative artists at critical junctures in their careers would bring their talents to the attention of a wider audience. Each exhibition was documented by a scholarly catalogue and traveled to museums nationwide.

Installation view of *Between Clouds of Memory: Akio Takamori, A Mid-Career Survey*, Arizona State University Art Museum, 2005

The Windgate Craft Initiative, which commenced in 2011 with funding from the Windgate Charitable Foundation, is an effort to reposition the ASU Art Museum as a major force in contemporary craft and create a new model of collecting, presenting, and generating information on contemporary craft within a broader art museum context. The Foundation provided the necessary resources to engage experts within Arizona State University and elsewhere to identify and prioritize initiatives that would advance craft scholarship and curatorial activities in academia and museums. The major components of the Windgate Craft Initiative are a visiting artist series; short- and long-term artist residences; and hiring a Windgate curatorial fellow to compile curatorial research and coordinate such activities as studio visits. The exhibition and catalogue *Crafting a Continuum: Rethinking Contemporary Craft,* and related acquisitions to the permanent collection in clay, wood, and fiber, primarily from emerging or under-recognized artists in these media, were also supported by this grant.

*Crafting a Continuum* advances the museum's commitment to present the craft field within the context of contemporary art. The acknowledgment of crafts as a significant and central part of the art world is an integral part of this initiative. While groundbreaking figures in the field are represented in depth, the museum feels it is also imperative to support under-recognized or emerging artists. They are the future.

1. Co-organized by The Forum, St Louis, Missouri, April 13–June 16, 1990.

2. Margo Shermeta, *Meeting Ground: Basketry Traditions and Sculptural Forms* (Tempe: ASU Art Museum, 1990), p. 4.

3. Linda Bills, Ken Carlson, Lillian Elliott, John Garrett, Pat Hickman, Kiyomi Iwata, Elizabeth Knowles, Dona Look, John McQueen, Norma Minkowitz, Jane Sauer, Kay Sekimachi and Frances Whitehead.

4. ASU Art Museum, Tempe, December 10, 2005–April 1, 2006; Houston Center for Contemporary Craft, Texas, June 29–September 23, 2007; Palo Alto Art Center, California, January 27–April 27, 2008; James A. Michener Art Museum, Doylestown, Pennsylvania, July 19–November 2, 2008; Bellevue Arts Museum, Washington December 17, 2008–March 22, 2009; New Mexico Museum of Art, Santa Fe, April 24–September 6, 2009, National symposia were held at ASU and Bellevue Arts Museum; New Mexico Museum of Art coordinated the exhibition and programs with SOFA.

5. Edward Jacobson, *Turned-Wood Bowls: A Gallery of Contemporary Masters—and More* (New York: E.P. Dutton, 1985), preface.

# THROWN OFF CENTER

## PERSONAL, COMMUNAL AND GLOBAL CERAMICS

Peter Held

THE CERAMICS FIELD HAS UNDERGONE A SEA CHANGE SINCE 1950, MARKED BY HIGH and low tides of critical discourse, and an ever-shifting reaction to the forces reshaping the clay world. Our vocabulary and conversations have evolved over time. Dramatic swings in studio practice, the marketplace, academia, collecting, and presenting have been introduced with each successive generation of artists. Given this history of generational shifts and the pervasive presence of technology today, much has changed. What can we expect to happen in the next decade? Where do we go from here?

The cyber speedway has accelerated the pace of change, and the rigid boundaries of craft are increasingly ruptured as the field is redefined by engagement with the wider worlds of visual arts and design. We have valued the history of ceramics and embraced its successes, but new ideas and technologies are rewriting the future.

Mexico City yarn-bombed bus, 2008, by textile artist and knit graffiti founder Magda Sayeg

Globalization, social networking, and commodity culture are other important forces influencing our cultural and social landscapes and reshaping what it means to be a ceramic artist in the twenty-first century. The Internet has leveled the playing field between cultures, while greatly expanded opportunities for international residencies have created new alliances in this shrinking world. These porous borders have opened pathways to previously uncharted territories, forging a broader and more inclusive perspective among artists and cultural presenters. Artists are increasingly taking on larger roles, becoming transdisciplinary knowledge producers. By mediating and exchanging new cultural models while building dialogues with shareholders who are marginalized or ignored, contemporary artists have expanded and invigorated mainstream culture.

These paradigms are shifting manifestations of sociopolitical, technological, economic, and cultural conditions in the contemporary world. Emerging clay practitioners are compelled to incorporate real world thinking into their socially engaged practices, whether motivated by private concerns, political activism, or collaboration with other artists. They are erecting their own structures of communication and distribution, creating horizontal rather than vertical hierarchies. They seek connectedness through social media, blogging, and podcasts, and becoming networked into design partnerships and DIY communities—the Do-it-yourself subculture of artists not formally trained in academia.

With the decentralization of clay, the classically trained craft-centered artist no longer has primacy, or, at least, not exclusive dominance. Conceptual art in the 1960s and 70s encouraged artists to work in a variety of mediums, applying individual style to whatever artistic opportunities were presented. This antagonized many formally trained ceramicists, who viewed these artists who crossed over into clay from the broader contemporary arts as interlopers and part-time visitors who were uneducated in craft traditions. They were suspected of being

Francesca DiMattio
*Jingdezhen*, 2012
Porcelain, china paint, underglaze
Courtesy of the artist and Salon 94
Gallery, New York
16 x 12½ x 12 in.

unaware of and having little interest in craft history. But these crossover artists, whether they are painters, video artists, or installation artists, bring a renewed vigor and aesthetic to the clay world. Francesca DiMattio, a painter in New York primarily known for her large-scale canvases, has taken architecture and interiors as subjects as a means of altering the concept of space. Her recent foray into ceramics juxtaposes and remixes a spectrum of historical associations and surface motifs; one style does not trump another, breaking down hierarchies of taste, value, and cultural specificity. Her vases respond to Peter Voulkos's slashed and torn vessels from the 1960s, delivering a potent, postfeminist decorative punch to the conventions of ceramics.

By addressing contemporary issues that impact new artistic practices, curators can encourage innovation, broaden the range of exhibition possibilities, and engage communities in new and exciting ways. The changing role of a curator—from a custodian of objects to a producer of meaning—has resulted in collaborative and interactive approaches, utilizing gallery spaces more as research laboratories than static showcases. Curators finding new platforms have become engaged with pressing issues affecting the communities they serve. As cultural entrepreneurs and knowledge producers, curators are catalysts for change.

Installation view of *Native Confluence: Sustaining Cultures*, 2009. Participating artists included Postcommodity, Nora Naranjo-Morse, and Bill and Athena Steen.

## FROM ICEHOUSE TO HOTHAUS:
## NEW ACQUISITIONS FROM DENMARK AND SWEDEN

Historically, Scandinavian ceramics has played an important role in applied arts and design. American audiences have had several opportunities to see firsthand museum exhibitions showcasing the range of approaches in this work: *Danish Ceramic Design* (1982) and *From the Kilns of Denmark* (2002) are two notable exhibitions that increased awareness among American audiences.[1] More recently, *Voices: Contemporary Ceramic Art from Sweden*, curated in 2008 by Stockholm gallerist Inger Molin, has brought wider exposure of these artists' work.[2] In the last ten years, there has been a growing trend of international art fairs, with many of the leading Scandinavian ceramic artists represented by gallerists, which has broadened their markets and recognition. American gallerists and collectors have responded with enthusiasm to work ranging from functional ceramics to cutting-edge sculpture.

Harbor view at Svaneke, Bornholm Island, Denmark, 2012.

In preparation for this exhibition, I spent three bone-chilling yet exhilarating weeks in December, 2012, traveling throughout Denmark and Sweden, visiting artists' studios, meeting curators and academics, and viewing museum exhibitions. The most enduring result of my experience is nine new acquisitions for the collection, which are included in this volume. I was instantly struck by the vast differences between how the clay and craft communities operate in the U.S. and Scandinavia, especially by the greater support the European governments (state and municipal) provide through free education, subsidized studio space, travel grants, and public art commissions. Applied art and design theory is also being advanced through innovative academic programs at Konstfack University College of Arts, Crafts and Design (Stockholm); The School of Design, Bornholm (Nexø), part of the Royal Danish Academy of Fine Arts in Copenhagen; and HDK: School of Design and Crafts, University of Göteborg, Sweden.

*We Work In A Fragile Material* is a craft-based design group that was founded in 2001 with the motivation and desire to broaden the perception of contemporary crafts. Many of its members, depicted below, attended Konstfack, Stockholm's School of Craft and Design.

I became better acquainted with the activities of THINK TANK, an independent pan-European group that, by disseminating information through writings, publications, and organizing innovative exhibitions, has been leading the way for craft theorists worldwide in interdisciplinary approaches toward craft. The nine theorists, curators, and makers of THINK TANK meet periodically to discuss changing roles in the applied arts, the relationship between craft and technology, and the aesthetic and social significance of the craft field in Europe. Their groundbreaking endeavors have had an impact on how I perceive and evaluate craft objects.[3]

Both curators and makers in northern Europe seemed more comfortable than American colleagues with interdisciplinary approaches and accelerated methodologies that examine materials, seeking embedded social and historical meanings inherent in physical attributes. Being incubated in a culture that simultaneously values both handwork and industrial design engenders spirited discourse and a high level of investigative research. Foraging from myriad artistic impulses, a new generation of makers in Denmark and Sweden is fostering a dynamic exchange of ideas among peers.

Stockholm-based artists and curators Zandra Ahl and Päivi Ernkvist coined the term "crafted form," to explain a specific movement. Crafted form cannot be defined as design, craft, or art but is a phenomenon that is in constant dialogue with these genres. Whereas techniques and materials have traditionally been valued (and even romanticized) in applied arts and crafts, crafted form emphasizes communication, discussion of issues, and experimental manufacturing processes.[4]

Objects carry power beyond their immediate use. They become iconic when they transmit shared stories, symbolic acts revealing an upheaval and reevaluation of social and cultural values. The makers I met embraced their rich cultural and artistic heritage in the applied and decorative arts and its close association with industry and the mass market. Many of these artists have diverse studio practices—variously, making one-off objects, designing for industry, curating, and executing public art commissions. The majority share studio space with other artists (mostly with former classmates) or work in collectives, such as We Work in a Fragile Material, a craft-based design group founded in 2001 in Stockholm by graduates of Konstfack. This sharing, driven in part by economic necessity and space constraints in urban areas, fosters philosophical alignments and reinforces cultural communitarianism.

The Copenhagen studio of Karen Kjæeldgård-Larsen (b. 1974) and Tine Broksø (b. 1971), who have been collaborators since 2000, is a hothouse, an environment conducive for nurturing

growth and spirited conceptual development. As the Claydies (Clay + Ladies = Claydies), Kjæeldgård-Larsen and Broksø operate in a contradictory, humorously associative, and opinion-forming universe, using clay in Dada-like performances, limited-production designs for industry, and one-off work. Their *True Feelings* series, a line of porcelain tableware that is pinch-formed while blindfolded, is guided by their manifesto that prohibits the use of tools, allowing them to work solely with their instincts of touch. The immediacy and tactility of *True Feelings* upends visual principles of ceramic design and offers critical commentary on the sterility of mass-produced objects.

Copenhagen-based artist Steen Ipsen (b. 1966) incorporates cording in his ceramics to create a sense of visual constriction. Ipsen's recent series *Tied-Up* is constructed from repeated molecular forms with monochromatic, high-gloss finishes bound by contrasting red cord, that are at once sensuous and constricted. Striving for graphic simplicity and geometric abstraction, Ipsen creates works that are rooted in modernist aesthetics and compatible with architecture and interior design. He explains:

> The works are structured and constructed, following certain rules. Elements of form are repeated and combined according to geometric systems or organic and mineral growth principles, such as cell division, gemmation and crystallization. For me, it's very much about the relation between methodical and chaotic, simple and complex.[5]

Gustaf Nordenskiöld (b. 1966, Swedish) has a diversified studio practice, combining fashion design, product development, and individual work that address issues of functionality, primitivism, and natural forces. Moving freely in his explorations between the fields of craft, design, arts, and industrial production, he challenges the conventions of beauty and the grotesque. Testing widely accepted concepts of Scandinavian minimal design and emphasis on the handmade, he employs both industrial processes and handwork, striving to break down hierarchies between the two. His webbed basketlike *Mure*, 2011, acknowledges utility and the plasticity of clay while inferring the tensions of everyday life. The taut climbing rope tethers the extruded tubes in place: without it, function fails.

Anders Ruhwald (b. 1974, Danish) makes sculptures that are disturbingly familiar yet unearthly; his gestating cocoon-like forms are glazed with hot, acidic colors. *Form and Function #2* and *You Are Here, This Is It*, both 2006, perch awkwardly on tubular metal legs, projecting an ambiguity that makes the viewer uneasy. The mutated works communicate his mastery of materials and prompt us to freely associate for meaning. Ruhwald's ongoing quest to understand the role objects play in our lives, the physical space they inhabit, and their social signifiers, poses the question of how we define ourselves in a world filled with things.

Anders Ruhwald
*Form and Function, #2*, 2006
Glazed earthenware, painted steel, piping, rubber caps
30 x 40 x 28 in.

The natural environment is the subject of Mia Göransson's (b. 1961, Swedish) ceramics. She uses grids with repetitive hard edges that are modulated with organic vegetation to reveal the delicate interplay between nature and humans. *New Nature: Squares of Nature*, 2012, is comprised of 400 squares of bone china, with leafy, wavelike patterns that are cast then hand-formed: it is ethereal in its translucency and refined craftsmanship. But the tinge of toxic yellow that makes *New Nature* glow evokes the continual degradation of the environment and our unwillingness to heed its warnings.

Mia Göransson
*Squares of Nature*, 2012 (detail)
Glazed porcelain

Karin Karinson Nilsson (b. 1970, Swedish) makes visceral sculptures that are a mash-up of readymades and hand-formed objects, a fluxing of clay, glaze, and glass coalescing into an amalgam of cultural relics embedded with associations both symbolic and metaphoric. In *This Was Not a Sneak Attack*, 2012, dainty creamers spew viscous, cascading ooze in a cultural accumulation flash frozen in time. Her art concerns mass-produced objects with little material or monetary value. Consumed by a society that perceives their aesthetic expression as tasteless or kitsch, the objects nonetheless conjure strong feelings of recognition, bringing personal and cultural associations and narratives to the viewer.

> My sculptures embody the symbolic, aesthetic, and cultural values that the objects in themselves possess, but by transferring these objects to alternative contexts I create contradictions and challenge the normative view. I want to raise questions that revolve around tradition. What happens when you move away from these traditions? And what happens in the encounter between spectator and object when the object no longer looks as expected?[6]

Per B. Sundberg
*The Gathering*, 2011 (detail)
Glazed porcelain, found objects

Per B. Sundberg (b. 1964, Swedish) is legendary (or even notorious) as an artist, former Konstfack professor, and the designer who developed new techniques at the famed Orrefors Glassworks (1994–2005), including the Fabula process of applying decals to a sub-layer, which were then covered with transparent glass. He incorporates readymades into his hand-built base structures, creating subversive and humorous tableaux, often in imagined landscapes. His G-Studio, located in a building formerly occupied by the Gustavsberg porcelain factory, was visually arresting—a Disneyesque world teeming with ceramic kitsch and detritus from flea markets and thrift shops. *The Gathering*, 2011, is a perverse menagerie of

Louise Hindsgavl
*The Required Action*, 2010 (detail)
Porcelain, mixed media

animals perched on a lumpen base. Breaking down commonly held assumptions about high and low art, class and taste, Sundberg, with his quick wit, thumbs his nose at Scandinavian "good design."

Sculptor Louise Hindsgavl (b. 1970, Danish) uses refined modeling and the seductiveness of porcelain to lure viewers closer and get them to unpack the fictive narratives in *The Required Action*, 2010. Because of the sculpture's brilliancy, the viewer must look for details and stitch together a story line within the fantastic—and, on closer inspection—disturbing tableau. It's an effective foil once you unravel its gruesome tale: a heap of vivisected animals and centaurlike creatures look uneasily toward a wholesome looking youth, armed with a hatchet. A trio of bound ducklings dangles from the uppermost branch as a centaur stretches menacingly for them. Influenced by surrealism and early folk tales, Hindsgavl mines our subconscious, delving into our dreams and buried desires in the battle of man versus beast.

## ACQUISITIONS: HERE AND NOW

Acquisition funds provided by the Windgate Craft Initiative, a multifaceted grant to elevate the museum's ongoing activities in the craft field, gave the museum curators the opportunity to purchase works by artists that they felt created a snapshot of current directions in the field. In doing so, the permanent collection now mirrors contemporary movements that were heretofore underrepresented. Both Paul Scott (b. 1953, British) and Del Harrow (b. 1977, American) utilize new computer-assisted technologies in their practice. By incorporating and adapting existing industrial processes, ceramic artists can now design an object on the computer and have a model quickly replicated by machine. Fab Labs with rapid prototyping, CNC routers, and 3-D laser cutters are mechanized innovations that have become de rigueur in academic programs, redefining the boundaries between the digital and analog worlds, while expanding makers' potential to create more complex forms.

Paul Scott
*Scott's Cumbrian Blue(s)- A Willow for Ai Weiwei, Wen Tao, Liu Zhenggang, Zhang Jinsong, Hu Mingfen,* 2011 (detail)
Found object (porcelain, c. 1840), decals

Del Harrow
*Cabinet # 3*, 2012
Porcelain, luster, wood
30 x 60 x 24 in.

Scott is a pioneering researcher of printing applications to ceramics, who draws on a wealth of historical and contextual investigations. *Cumbrian Blue(s)—A Willow for Ai Weiwei, Wen Tao, Liu Zhenggang, Zhang Jinsong, Hu Mingfen,* 2011, commemorates the political detention and ongoing harassment of the Chinese artist Ai Weiwei and his collaborators—a journalist, an architect, studio assistants, and family members—who have assisted him in prodding the government for expanded rights to freedom of speech. *Cumbrian Blue(s),* his series of blue-and-white decorated porcelain plates, alters the meaning of the original by overlay decoration on top of manufactured or existing surface decoration of the work and confounds originality and virtuality.

Harrow's *Cabinet # 3*, 2012, a *wunderkammer* of twenty-first–century artifacts, has its genesis in computer software. It is informed by his interests in both architectural spaces and complex fractal geometries inspired by nature, and is supplemented by his research in additive and subtractive manufacturing technologies. The arrangement of objects in this digitized still life, built bit by byte, is mitigated with evidence of the hand; its stippled, sanded, and scored planes add a nuanced surface that softens the mechanics of the process.

Linda Sormin (b. 1971, Thailand) has lived as a nomad, a global citizen who deals with issues of displacement, fragility, and instability. *Wanli*, 2010, a spatially precarious and un-

stable labyrinth of pinched coils and shards, references an eponymous ship wrecked circa 1625 and located in 2003. A Portuguese-owned ship built by Chinese laborers in India, the *Wanli* was laden with a large amount of high-quality porcelain ware from Jingdezhen, China, when it sank off the coast of Malaysia. The cause of the demise of the ill-fated voyage remains a mystery. Sormin's helter-skelter *Wanli*, places us in both the past and present, offering a glimpse of an inconstant future. Site-specific embedded memories become an important aspect of the work, addressing issues of commodity, labor, and cultural capital. For Sormin, the larger issues are trade, colonialism, and cultural hierarchies.

19

When facing mortality, one must fully come to terms with death. At our last moment and in periods of crisis, we may hope this fleeting time of recognition leads to acceptance. The Danish poet/philosopher Søren Kierkegaard found this hope persuasive, writing, "Instinctively, as do the shipwrecked, he will look around for something to which to cling, and that tragic, ruthless glance, absolutely sincere, because it is a question of his salvation, will cause him to bring order into the chaos of his life. These are the only genuine ideas; the ideas of the shipwrecked."[7] Can clay artists look upon the wreck *Wanli* as a metaphor for the future of craft? Precious cargo from the past is lost in storming seas, and years later its treasures are salvaged by new mariners. Adrift in new realities of shifting tides, ceramics must now traverse the porous borders of art, craft, and life.

Makers from diverse backgrounds and disciplines share insights as they collectively confront complex problems. While meeting innumerable challenges and opportunities, artists offer the potential of new discoveries. Precariously traversing a creative tightrope on the path to self-knowledge, makers mark the risks along the way. With sensitivity to material, infused with intellectual substance, craft becomes an effective means of communication, shedding light on our past, present, and future endeavors. The trajectory of our path forward is inexplicitly woven into life's tidal movements. We are in a state of flux, often thrown off center, but reside in a fertile moment with the future still in our grasp.

Linda Sormin
*Wanli*, 2010, (detail)
Glazed earthenware, found objects
(metal ship, porcelain shards from
dish by Sanam Emami)

1. The exhibition *Danish Ceramic Design* featured forty-five contemporary Danish artists and was curated by William Hull, former director of the Museum of Art, Pennsylvania State University, which organized the exhibition. The exhibition traveled to four museum venues. Danish Ceramic Design, exh. cat., text by William Hull (University Park: Museum of Art, Pennsylvania State University, 1981).
Curated by Wendy Tarlow Kaplan and Hope Barkan, *From the Kilns of Denmark: Contemporary Danish Ceramics* was a traveling exhibition first shown at the American Craft Museum in New York. Wendy Tarlow Kaplan and Hope Barkan, eds., *From the Kilns of Denmark: Contemporary Danish Ceramics,* exh. cat. (Copenhagen: Rhodos, 2002).

2. *Voices: Contemporary Ceramic Art from Sweden* featured ten pioneering Swedish ceramic artists and traveled to several U.S. museums. Sara Danius, Patrik Johansson, Galleri Inger Molin, *Samtida Svensk Keramisk Konst/ Voices: Contemporary Ceramic Art from Sweden* exhibition catalogue (Stockholm: Carlsson Bokförlag, 2006).

3. Founded in 2004, current THINK TANK members include: Dr. Peter Assmann, Linz, Austria; Liesbeth den Besten, Amstelveen, Netherlands; Gabi Dewald, Lorsch, Germany; Mònica Gaspar, Barcelona, Spain and Zürich, Switzerland; Dr. Tanya Harrod, London, Great Britain; Love Jönsson, Göteborg, Sweden, Dr. Louise Mazanti, Copenhagen, Denmark; Prof. Dr. Jorunn Veiteberg, Bergen, Norway and Copenhagen, Denmark; and Prof. Edmund de Waal, London, Great Britain. For more information regarding their activities go to their website at http://www.thinktank04.eu/home.php.

4. Zandra Ahl and Päivi Ernkvist, ed., *Formhantverk: Fortsättningsboken, Praktik och Reflektion* [Crafted Form: Continuation, Praxis and Reflection], (Stockholm: Vulkan, 2008).

5. Steen Ipsen, "Press Release," http://www.pulsceramics.com/exhibitions/steen-ipsen/press/ Accessed June 30, 2013.

6. Karin Karinson Nilsson, "Biography," http://www.mindysolomon.com. Accessed April 12, 2013.

7. Ernest Becker, *The Denial of Death* (New York: Free Press, 1973), 89.

Heather Sealy Lineberry

CRAFTING A CONTINUUM PROVIDED THE OPPORTUNITY FOR THE ASU ART MUSEUM to examine its contemporary craft collections and programs at a time of expanding scholarship and concurrent shifts in perspectives among artists. Recent publications, exhibitions, and symposia have filled gaps or revised the history of craft, and posited theoretical arguments on the definition of craft in the postmodern era and the impact of new technologies as tools and as dominant social systems.

Windgate Artist-in-residence Matthias Pliessnig demonstrates steam bent wood techniques with wood students from the ASU Herberger Institute for Design and the Arts, School of Art, 2012.

As a contemporary art museum in a university setting, our goal is to facilitate and participate in new research by artists, whether conceptual or material, and engage our students and public in the process by presenting and collecting works that encapsulate this experimentation. Our programming has moved fluidly between craft and craft-like, to use Jenni Sorkin's terminology,[1] presenting contemporary artists who explore the media, processes, or ideas of craft from different starting points and with different intentions. This range is echoed by our curators, who are both media specific and broadly curating in contemporary art; by our exhibitions, individually or collectively in a season; and by our collections. We are an unusual contemporary art museum in our embrace of art forms that range from functional ceramics to performance and social practice completely divorced from the object. Such breadth could be unfocused, but its expansiveness presents opportunities for a dialogic relationship between art and craft and a more powerful investigation of the broader cultural and social terrain.

In recent years our collecting in wood and fiber has focused on diverse processes, international artists, and approaches intersecting with the history of sculpture. As described in the preface, the ASU Art Museum's wood collection is grounded in the historically important Jacobson Collection of turned-wood bowls. The fiber collection, smaller and recent in its formation, is strongest in baskets and dimensional forms. Our selections from the fiber and wood collections for *Crafting a Continuum* begin in the 1980s, and, not surprisingly, the work from this decade and the 90s is dominated by these starting points and by studio craft. Predominantly vessel forms and domestic in scale, these objects reveal experimentation by artists in their studios with materials and traditional techniques. Among the exceptional artists included are Ed Rossbach, Dorothy Gill Barnes, David Ellsworth, Lillian Elliott, Stephen Hogbin, Ed and Philip Moulthrop, John Garrett, and Jerry Bleem, to name a few.

Installation view, *Turning Point: Inspired by the Edward Jacobson Collection of Turned Wood Bowls*, 2006

Two pieces from these early decades clearly demonstrate hybrid approaches that sample widely from craft and sculpture traditions and set the tone for the future: Tom Eckert's *MM-342 (Tank Chair)* from 1980 and John McQueen's *Cultivar "a tree can't but be"* from 1992. Eckert, our colleague at Arizona State University, works with wood not for its "intrinsic beauty and personality" but for its flexibility.[2] There is no limit to what he can make out of wood. He talks about skill as a vehicle for expression, whether to capture beauty or awe or to convey complicated content, as in this early piece that pairs a chair with a tank and questions the prevalence of violence and war. McQueen trained as a sculptor and embraced basket making for what he considered to be its more open-ended possibilities. Selected from a number of McQueen works in the ASU Art Museum collection, *Cultivar* is a monumental tree-like object constructed from plywood and screws and ringed by poetic text.

The fiber and wood selections from 2000 to today are dominated by new acquisitions, which are the focus of this essay, yet the existing works in the collection already signal changes, straddle perceived art and craft divisions, and include international artists. Sculptural works by Connie Mississippi and Robyn Horn demonstrate the establishment of women in the traditionally male-dominated field of wood turning and woodworking (as does Virginia Dotson's 1992 vessel from the *Wind Eye* series). Efrain Almeida and Jarbas Lopes are Brazilian artists who draw upon—or appropriate—wood-carving and basket traditions. Claudette Schreuders from South Africa is influenced by African and European wood-carving traditions in her diminutive, figurative works that convey arresting social and political narratives.

Installation view, *The Long Day: Sculpture by Claudette Schreuders*, 2004

Keeping in mind the existing collections in wood and fiber, Elizabeth Kozlowski and I contacted artists, curators, and educators for recommendations on artists who are producing innovative work; we visited studios and museums, both large city museums with contemporary craft departments and smaller focused institutions; we attended conferences and gathered publications. We identified several artists who were expansive and distinctive in their practice of working with wood and fiber. Mark Newport and Sonya Clark stand out in our selections as important teachers at Cranbrook and Virginia Commonwealth University, respectively, who are influencing a generation of artists and still find time to create powerful bodies of work. Newport embroiders comic book covers and knits superhero costumes. *W Man* is a superhero of the artist's devising, part of a series that represents the essential elements: earth, air, fire, and water. Newport started knitting the costumes after becoming a father, which he found intensified his male identity, whether internally or externally defined. While they have been worn by the artist in (often private) performances, the suits hang limply in the gallery space, raising issues of masculinity, heroism, nurture, and protection. Clark's well-known body of work uses combs bound together in wall hangings and free-standing works to consider the legacy of utility in craft and expand the definition of fiber and weaving. In *Threadwrapped in Blue and Brown,* the combs are wrapped in a style similar to West African hairstyles and arranged in strips to resemble both a flag and traditional West African woven cloth. Clark has a deep interest in the content intrinsic to materials and she plumbs this common object—the comb—for its role in African American history, race politics, and social perceptions of hair.

John McQueen
*CULTIVAR "a tree can't but be,"* 1992
Plywood, screws
60 x 24 x 7 in.

Alison Elizabeth Taylor studied graphics and then painting before discovering marquetry—much has been written about her inspiration for turning to this exacting and historic medium.[3] Taylor manages to create fluid images with this exacting and technique of piecing together wood veneers and adhering them to a flat matrix. Her subjects and sites are enhanced by the tension between the tangible, material surface and the illusion of space. *Chainlink*, 2008, is a close-up of a drained, dilapidated, and fenced pool at a motel at the Salton Sea, a failed resort now inhabited by loaners and drifters. This scene was all too familiar in Phoenix suburbs during the recent recession and is a pointed example of the shifting meaning of artworks due to context and viewers' experiences. Taylor's next body of work actually focused on foreclosures, with imagery drawn from time spent with a Las Vegas repo man.

The artists represented by new acquisitions, including Taylor, seem genuinely unconcerned by how their work is classified. They are forty or younger, with advanced degrees from universities. Most studied in fiber or furniture programs and consider this a starting point for their transdisciplinary work. They are informed and knowledgeable about the debates: whether we should abandon the word craft and all its baggage, as Glenn Adamson has suggested,[4] or whether it makes sense to make objects by hand in 2013. These younger artists are focused on building their skills, working with their chosen material, pursuing their concepts, building their networks, and securing the next residency or visiting lecturer position. As Matthias Pliessnig and Christine Lee write in their statements included in this catalog, and visiting artist Nao Matsunaga said in his lecture, they emphasize and value skill and admire it in others. They are convinced by the power of the handmade object, citing centuries of human fascination, and they express concern for overemphasis on the digital, even as

Nao Matsunaga, a Windgate Artist-in-residence, working at the graduate ceramic studio at ASU, 2013.

they draw upon new technologies in their making and their careers.

David Rowe and Katie Hudnall use scrap and discarded wood in their work to convey age and use. Rowe's diorama-like reliefs are inspired by abandoned industrial landscapes from the artist's Midwestern home—timely stories of the rise and fall of industry. Just as these landscapes in their dissipation have a romantic appeal, Rowe's works have a push-pull sensibility in their monumental scale and detailed construction, pattern, and color. Hudnall uses her great skills in joinery to construct modern-day reliquaries or curiosity cabinets from discarded and imperfect materials. Her *Bolt Reliquary* is a spindly contraption with kinetic fingers that painstakingly pull apart and reveal the venerated bolt inside. Is this a maker's appreciation for the simple but crucial mechanism, or a warning about our lack of familiarity with building things?

Yoshimasa Tsuchiya is a woodcarver who studied Buddhist sculpture and art conservation and designed video games before beginning a series of fantastical carved animals. The otherworldly, or what has been described as "newborn,"[5] quality to these works derives from a mix of influences—Japanese folklore, myths, dreams, art history, manga, and anime. The carved and stained figures, like *Carnival*, are sweet and aggressively repellent, restful and disturbingly present. While *Carnival* is an unidentifiable hybrid, some of Tsuchiya's animals quote specifically from Japanese folk traditions, although he often disrupts the reference with surprising shifts in scale or posture.

On first viewing, *Nopal #3*, by Margarita Cabrera, could be mistaken as part of the recent informal craft movement, artists using craft traditions in purposefully casual ways. Rather, the work reveals the rich, socially engaged practice that generated the piece, a deeply collaborative process that is as important as the final object. Cabrera, like many social practice artists, including Jarbas Lopes, mentioned above, is drawn to craft for its physical and emotional connectivity, rooted in history and making.[6] Sorkin has argued that the history of craft is based upon supportive, social networks, which continues to define the art form.[7] Social gathering and activism have a rich history in craft, from quilting bees to Judy Chicago's *Dinner Party* in the 1970s and *Birth Project* in the 1980s to DIY craft events.

Yoshimasa Tsuchiya
*Carnival*, 2005 (detail)
Hinoki (Japanese cypress), paint, crystals

Drawing upon her own history and working with border issues and communities, Cabrera uses traditional crafts from Mexico to bring immigrants together around their compelling, shared experiences of living in between cultures and economies. Cabrera's series of cacti, *Space in Between*, are created at workshops around the country where she collaborates with local immigrant organizations. (*Nopal #3* was produced at the McColl Center for the Visual Arts in Charlotte, NC, working with Escuela Bilingue). The fabric pads, made from Border Patrol uniforms, were embroidered by Mexican American immigrants using a visual language to tell their poignant stories of crossing the border.

LEFT
Katie Hudnall
*Bolt Reliquary*, 2011 (detail)
Cherrywood, boxwood, oak, mixed media

RIGHT
*Space In Between* is a collaborative project with Margarita Cabrera in the form of a sewing and embroidery workshop with local residents that took place at Box 13 Gallery in Houston, Texas.

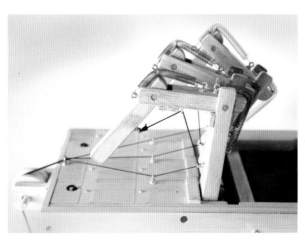

Matthias Pliessnig
*Brace,* 2012

Matthias Pliessnig trained in venerable furniture-making programs,[8] yet he talks about "fighting furniture" and "furniture as a vehicle to make objects." Inspired by Thonet's bentwood chair from the mid nineteenth century, specifically by that cabinetmaker's ability to make fluid a rigid material, Pliessnig has developed his own technique to bend wood to surprising extremes while maintaining the strength and stability of the piece. He uses the computer as a tool when creating preliminary drawings and then leaves it behind as he works by hand in an additive, freeform process in a rough mold, bending and forming the wood. *Brace,* 2012, was commissioned by the ASU Art Museum, and we encouraged him to take his freeform construction further. The resulting bench is a basket or nest or pod, surprisingly comfortable and visually striking.

So, what do we glean from this continuum of artists and objects gathered by the ASU Art Museum during the last few decades? Succinctly, that there is a rich hybrid practice in contemporary craft. The March 2013 issue of *Artforum* included an article by Jeffrey Weiss exploring the status of the object in the postmodern era, which has "given way in artistic practice to a mobile, variable, or indeterminate relation between the terms of a work and its material means."[9] While Weiss is specifically talking about the legacy of minimalism and conceptualism, and issues of dematerialization and authenticity related to fabrication, this "unfixed material identity of the aesthetic object" has become a rallying cry for artists and scholars to defend craft and the handmade object. Yet it is clear from our research and acquisitions that craft and the handmade object are not going away. Craft may wax or wane but it continues to be a touchstone. Despite concerns about a de-skilled society, many younger artists continue to value and perfect skill with their hands. Artists pursue their work with different toolboxes, employ new technologies in surprising ways, and roam freely through art, craft, and design to find what they need.

1. Jenni Sorkin, "Craft-like: The Illusion of Authenticity" (lecture, Nation Building: Craft and Contemporary American Culture, symposium at the Renwick Gallery, Smithsonian American Art Museum, Washington, DC, November 8–9, 2012). http://americanart.si.edu/renwick/symposium/ (accessed January 15, 2013).

2. Tom Eckert, interview by Jo Lauria, June 19, 2007, unpublished transcript, Archives of American Art, Smithsonian Institution. Other content from conversations between the author and artist in 2011.

3. *American Gothic: Aaron Spangler & Alison Elizabeth Taylor,* exhibition catalogue (Winston-Salem, NC: The Southeastern Center for Contemporary Art, 2011); *Kitty McManus Zurko, Alison Elizabeth Taylor,* exhibition catalogue (Wooster, OH: The College of Wooster Art Museum 2009);

4. Glenn Adamson, "Goodbye Craft," (keynote address, Nation Building: Craft and Contemporary American Culture, symposium at the Renwick Gallery, Smithsonian American Art Museum, Washington, DC, November 8–9, 2012). http://americanart.si.edu/renwick/symposium/ (accessed January 15, 2013).

5. Toshiaki Hozumi, "Yoshimasa Tsuchiya—The Very Reasons Why in a World of Silence," *Sylvan Whispers: Yoshimasa Tsuchiya,* exhibition catalogue (Tokyo: Megumi Ogita Gallery, 2012).

6. For a good survey of this trend, see Paula Owen, "Fabrication and Encounter: When Content is a Verb," in *Extra/Ordinary: Craft and Contemporary Art,* Maria Elena Buszek, ed. (Durham, NC: Duke University Press, 2011), 92.

7. Loc cit, Sorkin, "Craft-like: The Illusion of Authenticity."

8. Rhode Island School of Design, BFA, and the University of Wisconsin, MFA.

9. Jeffrey Weiss, "Things Not Necessarily Meant to be Viewed as Art," *Artforum* 51, no. 7 (March 2013): 221–229.

# CRAFT-IN-RESIDENCE

## THE OPEN STUDIO NETWORK

Jenni Sorkin

R ETHINKING CONTEMPORARY CRAFT SHOWCASES MEMBERS OF THREE GENERATIONS
of Americans and European practitioners, many of whom established deep and
lasting connections to alternative, non-academic training programs. These run the
gamut from rural schools like Haystack Mountain School of Crafts in Maine (founded
1950) and Penland School of Crafts in North Carolina (founded 1929) to urban community spaces like Greenwich House Pottery (founded 1902) and UrbanGlass (founded 1977,
both New York City). Rooted in community-building and non-competition, these sites, which
offer residencies, studio space, or a combination of the two, have been wrongly viewed as
supplements: augmentations to a traditional four-year degree program, considered to be
not as (or sufficiently) rigorous as academic training.

Yet these program sites have been crucial partners not only in advancing craft, but in
bridging craft's twentieth-century roots and its twenty-first–century future, forging crucial
relationships between artistic practice, pedagogy, and community participation. Not
beholden to either accreditation requirements or permanent faculty, these organizations
by their inherent flexibility continue to drive practice forward. "Craft-in-residence" evokes an
open studio or workshop: a live/work situation, or site-specific laboratory that encourages
production through skilled investigation. By citing and circumscribing the measured testing
and development of ideas within a controlled environment, residency programs emphasize
the importance of knowledge exchange, meaningful dialogue, and immersion in a particular skill set.

Artist-in-residence programs have fostered the deliberate spontaneity of craft-trained artists
who have expanded craft practices to include a vast array of new technologies, including
design, fabrication, and mixed-media practices imported from sculpture, installation, per-
formance, and video. Some offer a wide range of disciplines and media, such as Haystack
Mountain School of Crafts and Anderson Ranch Arts Center (founded 1973, Snowmass
Village, Colorado), while others are medium-specific programs like Pilchuck Glass Workshop (founded 1971, Stanwood, Washington), Archie Bray Foundation for the Ceramic
Arts (founded 1951, Helena, Montana), and Red Lodge Clay Center (founded 2005, Red
Lodge, Montana). The Kohler Arts/Industry Residency Program (founded 1974,
Sheboygan, Wisconsin) fosters the production of new work in an iron/brass
foundry and enamel shop.

The relatively fluid structure of seasonal and rotational programs, which are
unhampered by curriculum requirements, allows these sites to respond to new
directions in the field. Those with residency components in rural areas also offer
an immersive experience, degrees of financial support, and the time and space
necessary for intense concentration, where the distractions of contemporary life
are muted. While none are strictly post-graduate programs, many have morphed
into nearly obligatory way stations, stopovers on the path to permanent teaching
positions and solo exhibitions.

In the early postwar years, craft practice found a home in academia: throughout the United States, the GI Bill was the impetus for university-based initiatives
in manual arts and design, expanding college art departments at a rapid clip

Resident artist James McKinnell dem-
onstrating his wheel throwing skills
for community members. Archie Bray
Foundation, circa 1955.

throughout the late 1940s and into the 1950s. But such programs as blacksmithing, ceramics, jewelry, and glass require highly specialized equipment and purpose-built spaces that must pass exacting health and safety standards. In academic settings, they are often considered a liability. Even though the era of late-night drinking, bare feet, and lack of eye protection are vestiges of the past, these programs are perpetually in danger of being phased out at the whim of administrators who often have little understanding or sympathy for artistic, materials-based research.[1]

The recent dissolution of disciplinary boundaries and merging of crafts within contemporary art has reversed the fragmentation of the craft field that academia inadvertently supported by encouraging experimentation. It is no longer surprising to see current MFA students sewing on their paintings or make abstract sculptures in clay. Ceramists make videos; video artists toy with handmade objects. Few emerging artists define themselves by medium alone, but instead cultivate an identity rooted in the content of their artistic production. The relationship between an artist and his or her materials further morphs in the public sphere. In the current genre of social practice, the primary consideration is reciprocity between artist and audience; material often becomes a secondary consideration.

During the 1950s the laissez-faire craft-teaching style, epitomized by Peter Voulkos when he was at the helm of the famed Otis program, created momentum and a breakthrough in experimentation with forms and materials. In the freewheeling atmosphere at Otis, students including John Mason and Jerry Rothman were propelled toward large-scale non-utilitarian works. As a field, ceramics has been protective of the hard-won disciplinary advances that Voulkos and his students produced: the ability to reject functionalism altogether and create sculptural forms in clay. This experimentation was great for his students, and for some in generations after, like Robert Arneson and David Gihooly. For these latter ceramists working in the 1960s and 1970s, traditional throwing and firing techniques were required training, yet as they sought to undo the strictures of formal training, ceramics, and other craft disciplines, subsequently changed.

The full-scale embrace of interdisciplinary practice also has a darker reality: few student-artists of the 1990s, 2000s, and 2010s have graduated with a skill set deep enough to produce a sustained body of work or, in turn, to teach basic skills to undergraduates. The latter, after all, is what the academy wants, even if it claims otherwise. Post-graduate residency programs become the necessary next step, where an artist is able to work independently, but within a peer community, which provides the built-in audience that is so difficult to leave behind after a degree program. As well, skill acquisition becomes a necessity because there is no longer a lab tech present. This supported independence cultivates the confidence to master technique in a non-competitive environment, fostering a continued maturation in art making. The organizations of the past offer a pathway for the re-privileging of materiality, that is, a way to restore the skill set to what has become increasingly become a de-skilled practice.

The earliest craft schools were established in Appalachia: among them, Arrowmont School of Crafts in Gaitlinburg, Tennesee (1926), John C. Campbell Folk School in 1925 and Penland School of Crafts in 1929, both in North Carolina. A concerted effort by civic-minded women, private philanthropists, and such government agencies as the Women's Bureau of the Department of Labor coalesced to establish craft schools in order to develop highly skilled home workers, many of whom were women, thereby improving economic prospects in an economically depressed region of the country.[2] In urban settings, similar craft programs were based within settlement houses during the Progressive Era. The earliest of the settlement houses was also the most renowned: Hull House, founded in Chicago in 1889, became a model for innovative community-based programming and outreach. Close cooperation with the local neighborhood, or what founder Jane Addams called "residence," was one of the principles of her influential philosophy.[3]

Another wave of institutions was established after the war to provide something that was missing in local communities: studio or work space, a need for instruction, or a site that would foster and nourish the artistic aspirations and growth of a fledgling community. Haystack Mountain School of Crafts in Deer Isle, Maine (1950), Florida Craftsmen (1951, roaming

Peter Voulkos working in his Los Angeles, California, studio, circa 1959.

Warren MacKenzie conducting a workshop at Pottery Northwest, Seattle, Washington, circa 1975.

until 1986), Pond Farm in Guerneville, California (1958), and Pottery Northwest (1966, Seattle) were established during this period. The original craft schools of the South also updated and expanded their offerings during this era: Arrowmont initiated a summer craft workshops in 1945; the Campbell Folk School emphasized its non-competitive instruction and expanded its community events; and in 1962, Penland established its fellowship and three-year residency programs.[4] During the 1970s, as a craft-based response to the art world's alternative space movement, urban studio spaces proliferated: Clay Studio in Philadelphia (1974), Lillstreet Art Center in Chicago (1975), UrbanGlass in Brooklyn (1977), Clayworks Studio Workshop in New York (1979), and Baltimore Clayworks (1980). Steeped in experimentation and open work spaces, clay and glass were mediums especially conducive to the framework of a group dynamic and to concepts of change.

While mixed-media craft practices have become commonplace, medium specificity remains a constant in numerous time-limited summer programs. It is entirely within the purview of the alternative pedagogical craft circuit to revive specific skill sets, such as shibori, enameling, slip decoration, or wood joinery. Basketry, for instance, is a traditional art form that has largely been written off by degree-granting institutions, but has evolved through the efforts of numerous alternative institutions in the field, such as Arrowmont and Haystack, where Dorothy Gill Barnes (American, b. 1927), who makes sculptural and vessel forms in wood, regularly taught workshops on the use of natural materials, such as those found in her own work. *Coiled Banyan* (1988) looks like a very sophisticated nest, held together with interwoven strips of bark that double as a decorative device. At the Pacific Basin School of Textile Arts and Fiberworks, Center for Textile Arts, two distinct schools in Berkeley, California, founded in the early 1970s, fiber-based artists sought to explore and expand a repertoire of possibilities in textile practice. At Pacific Basin, Lillian Elliot (American, 1930–1994) and Pat Hickman (American, b. 1941) taught numerous courses on netting, vessel construction, and basketry. Fiberworks, established by Gyöngy Laky in 1973, offered advanced textile workshops by such artists as Ed Rossbach (American, 1914–2002), but also had a dedicated exhibition space for works in fiber, including ethnic and traditional textiles, at a time when Bay Area institutions largely ignored work in this medium. Laky described the impetus for displaying non-Western art:

> Automatically through this institution, we were reaching out to other cultures all over the world…Here it was, in 1974, in an area where there were many, many Chinese Americans living, and there had been no exhibitions of Chinese textiles [since 1944]. Chinese textiles are extraordinary. They're really very beautiful, very interesting, and done with enormous skill…So here we are heading into somewhere where, very naturally, the greatest inspiration is coming from the most disenfranchised groups around us…[5]

Joanne Segal Brandford (American, 1933–1994), whose *Basket-figure* (1983) was heavily influenced by Native American woven forms, was instrumental in pioneering the earliest History of Textiles course offered at UC Berkeley; she later (1972–1978) became a research fellow in textile art at the Peabody Museum of Archaeology and Ethnology at Harvard.[6] Cultural references make themselves apparent in Katherine Westphal's (American, b. 1919) *Cortes* (1995), a basket made of raffia and rubber that, through its materials, merges two symbols

Basket making workshop at Arrowmont School of Arts and Crafts, circa 1970s, unknown participants.

of colonization. Westphal uses plant sources associated with slave labor to create an ominous sculptural basket named for Hernán Cortés, the brutal conquistador responsible for overthrowing the Aztec Empire in Mexico in 1519. In *Japanese Plaited Basket* (1987), Rossbach used braiding techniques inspired by bamboo basketry, but incorporated non-traditional materials like staples and paper. More recently, Jerry Bleem (American, b. 1954) has utilized the detritus from offices—paper clips, rubber bands, and staples—as the raw materials of his basket forms. *Weight/Wait* (1998) incorporates business cards and sealing wax, perhaps embalming a custom that is on the wane in the digital age. Jarbas Lopes (Brazilian, b. 1964) has produced a hybrid form: *Cicloviaéra* (2006) is a sculpture that appropriates the leisure bicycle, complete with its requisite wicker basket. Fusing two disparate entities, the artist produced a wicker-covered bicycle, woven using traditional hard straw, that is offered to members of the public as a literal point of departure. Lopes's interest in social engagement, which is inspired by activist political movements, parallels Laky's recovery of ethnographic traditions by her generation, asserting that the medium of weaving—or any craft medium—can be an agent of change.

The open structure of residencies, which promote an informal network of exchange, is one catalyst for idealism about change. With its built-in peer group of fellow artists, who provide

camaraderie, support, and feedback at a critical early stage in an artist's career, the post-graduate residency is often where emerging artists discover their voices, create their first mature body of works, and find validation for their practices. This strong sense of community creates entrenched loyalties, where artists come back as board members, or take a permanent administrative position with the organization to insure their access to equipment, studio space, and a support system. The permanent link to residency programs is another key difference between studio craft, and its inheritors.

Jarbas Lopes
*Cicloviaéra*, 2006
Osier (natural fiber vine) over bicycle
42 x 72 x 20½ in.

Academic jobs, plentiful during the 1960s and 1970s, provided stability for studio crafts through that period, but that economic base is rarely available today. Now, many excellent artists are forced to cobble together residencies and adjunct teaching jobs for years on end, or have given up on the academy altogether, have decided to make a go of it themselves. Ceramist Marguerite Wildenhain (b. France, 1896–1985) always encouraged this self-sufficiency, warning that a craftsman could not afford to be dependent upon either the facilities or tools of the academy: instead to produce the best work, he or she must remain autonomous. Wildenhain's autonomy was also highly dependent upon a collector base, which has shrunk as collectors find themselves alienated and at odds with an increasingly fluid set of craft practices. At museums and private studios alike, this patron class has not regenerated itself easily or quickly; it is possible that is will never come back. So in this sense, studio craft dreamed up a model it could not itself sustain.

Beth Cavener Stichter (American, b. 1972) practices full-time as a studio artist, but she has spent a great deal of time in residency programs, including at the Archie Bray Foundation, the Clay Studio, and Pottery Northwest. Such fellowship programs have allowed her the time and space to create her large-scale ceramic sculptures, such as *Object Lesson: Apathy* (2003), in which a black goat resides in a permanent state of uncertainty, eyes wide, crouching on all fours in glass tank filled with water, only his snout pointed above the waterline. The work is angst-inducing, with the animal crammed into each inch of available space. Stichter says the narrowness of the kiln door at Archie Bray, prompted her to utilize this limitation in the works she developed there.[7]

Guy Michael Davis (American, b. 1979) and Katie Parker (American, b. 1980) collaborate and produce work under the moniker Future Retrieval. They have most recently completed a nine-month residency at the historic Rookwood Pottery in Cincinnati, and done several short residencies abroad, one together, in China, and others apart, in Poland and Germany. At the Pottery Workshop in Jingdezhen, China, the pair worked with local artisans to expand their knowledge of mold making and the properties of porcelain. *Hye-Que Monkey in Captivity* (2011) is one of five similarly hybrid works that showcases a small monkey at the center of a decorative oval frame, backed in vibrant red wallpaper, its color and patterning a screenprint appropriated from the fauna-rich background of *The Unicorn Tapestries* (1495–1505), medieval masterworks on permanent view at The Cloisters in upper Manhattan and the Musée Cluny in Paris. The monkey stands atop a pedestal and holds an artifact in its hands. Future Retrieval's foray into installation work is a way of recycling and merging disparate political histories, East-West craft traditions, symbolism, and decoration.

Andrew Casto
*Assemblage 44*, 2012 (detail)
Glazed ceramic, gold luster, paint, wood, metal

Future Retrieval:
Guy Michael Davis and Katie Parker
*Hye-Que Monkey in Captivity*, 2011
(detail)
Glazed porcelain, screenprint, wood

sculptures into full-scale installations during a long-term residency at Archie Bray from 2011 until 2013. His presentation diminishes any lingering preciousness: his sculptures swing precariously from neon yellow cables, perch at odd angles from wooden shelving, and seem to defy gravity in chaotic growth spurts, with chunky appendages and half-formed protuberances. His organic forms—something that hovers between a spore growing a spiky, beautiful fungus and an artificial rock made for a natural history display—play with biomorphism while mapping the human appetite for geological formations and exploration, which is also a way of experiencing or marking time. We often perceive the deep time of geology to be nearly impossible to grasp. Casto's work trades in the traveler's impulse to visit to caverns, caves, and tawdry highway "wonderspots," and is, at base, a low-level search for a taste of the vastness of the universe and its slow changes over many millennia.

Many of these aforementioned residency programs and places function on different registers from the majority culture in the United States. They are aimed not only at emerging and established artists, but also at numerous amateur and at-risk populations, ranging from kids to adults, who can benefit from thoughtful and targeted programming. Programs like Community Arts at Baltimore Clayworks collaborate with area service providers and nonprofits to offer arts education to low-income and marginalized populations. Haystack offers a number of enrichment opportunities to similar populations in Maine, and has expanded its scholarship program and the number of paid teaching assistants. These social commitments reflect craft's roots in community and veteran affairs. This legacy of community building allows for an expansive understanding of craft, which is defined less as an object than as a network.

To pass through any of these sites, or hubs, is to become inducted into, or networked into, the culture of studio craft. Broadly construed, this network of pedagogical sites, situations, and institutions defines studio craft. This misreading of studio craft practice, which ties the object to the maker from production to market, is purposeful. In rethinking craft practices, if our definitions expand toward the democratic and populist, rather than exquisitely singular, craft has perhaps come full circle.

1. Medium-specific departments and programs are closing with increasing regularity: Maryland Institute College of Art announced the closure of its jewelry program in 2012. MICA's website reads: "As of December 2012, the School for Professional and Continuing Studies is no longer accepting new applications to the Jewelry Certificate." http://www. mica.edu/Programs_of_Study/School_for_Professional_and_Continuing_Studies/Certificate_in_Jewelry.html. Accessed January 16, 2013.
This is not just an American phenomenon either: The British Crafts Council tracked the following closures throughout the United Kingdom, mainly in glass and ceramics:
Goldsmiths College, University of London: MA ceramics (closed 1993)
Goldsmith College, University of London: MA textiles (closed 2010)
Camberwell College of Art: textiles BA (closed 1993)
Camberwell College of Art: metal and jewelry BA (closed 2006)
City Lit: stained glass course (closed 2005)
Staffordshire University: glass department (closed 2006)
Manchester Metropolitan University: contemporary applied arts BA (closed 2007)
Glasgow School of Art: ceramics department (closed 2008)
Duncan of Jordanstone College of Art, University of Dundee: ceramics department (date unknown)
http://www.craftscouncil.org.uk/about-us/press-room/view/2009/briefing-notes-number-one

2. The Hunter Library of Western Carolina University, Cullowhee, NC, has created an excellent website from their extensive archives. See "Craft Revival: Shaping Western North Carolina Past and Present", www.wcu.edu/craftrevival/index.html. See also Jane S. Becker, *Selling Tradition: Appalachia and the Construction of an American Folk, 1930-1940* (Chapel Hill: The University of North Carolina Press, 1998).

3. Louise C. Wade, "The Heritage from Chicago's Early Settlement Houses," *Journal of the Illinois State Historical Society* 60, no. 4 (Winter 1967), 414.

4. See the history section of the John C. Campbell Folk School's website: www.folkschool.org.

5. Harriet Nathan, "Fiber Art: Visual Thinking and the Intelligent Hand." Oral History with Gyöngy Laky, Berkeley, CA: Regional Oral History Office, Bancroft Library. See also Barbara Goldberg, "Joanne Segal Brandford" in T*extile Society of America Symposium Proceedings* (2004), Paper 450, 202–209. http://digitalcommons.unl.edu/tsaconf/450 (accessed January 13, 2013)

6. Goldberg, ibid, 202–209.

7. Beth Cavener Stichter, "Cornered Rabbit," http://www.followtheblackrabbit.com/Cornered_Rabbit.html. Accessed January 13, 2013.

# THE TIME OF THE OBJECT

Synnøve Vik

THE QUESTION "IN WHAT TIME DO WE LIVE?" EVOKES NOTIONS OF CONTEMPORANEITY, nostalgia and—perhaps inevitably at a time where economic and environmental apocalypse seems to hover in a not-so-distant future—both utopia and dystopia.[1] One way to understand our current time is to come to terms with the notion of the object and our perception of its production. Things, objects, material artifacts made by hand or by machines are at the crux of our practical lives, and our fantasies. This fact connects our sense of craft and its qualities to currents and trends in society at large. When everything is globalized and all kinds of goods are easily available, what is craft's place in the culture at large, as a material, tangible practice, and related to other kinds of things and artistic practices? However—and this might seem quite contradictory—we also live in the time of the immaterial, where communication flows freely, uninhibited by material boundaries. Material objects make this fluid communication possible. The present time is immaterial in a particularly material sense.

Caroline Roux, acting editor at *Crafts Magazine*, has written: "Craft has never been more important than now, as an antidote to mass production and as a practice in which the very time it takes to produce an object becomes part of its value in a world that often moves too fast."[2] As much as Roux is right, this oversimplifies the current situation. Craft is not an antidote to mass production as much as it makes visible a production process that is no longer evident in most developed countries, due to outsourcing. Craft upholds certain connections between materials, processes, and objects that seem to be missing in these immaterial times. The philosopher Jacques Rancière sees the fundamental conflict of politics not as a struggle between opposing interests but as a struggle for access to the shared social sphere – the community. This struggle takes place through what he calls the distribution of the sensible, "the dividing-up of the world and of people."[3] The distribution of the sensible reveals, for example, who are considered proper subjects of the community, and what is seen as relevant to the community. Craft brings the question of production, the conditions for its execution, and value of the outcome, into the view of our community.

Artisan creating handcrafted silk ties for the French fashion house Hermès.

To establish the relevance of craft in a globalized society, one must first acknowledge that the meaning of this term varies widely not only from country to country, but more importantly between the Northwestern and Southeastern parts of the world. These localized attitudes reflect different traditions and the extent to which craft has been aligned to art or handicraft. I choose to narrow my perspective, defining craft as a form of art based in knowledge of a material process, that is, an artist—or rather, craft-artist—thinking with his hands and through a material as well as with his head.

## THE SPELL OF CRAFTSMANSHIP

The long period of excitement over the possibilities that were created by digital exploration and expansion has been supplanted by nostalgia for the analogue.[4] We have come to realize that the digital world is always reliant upon material objects, that objects are being developed and discarded at increasingly high speeds. While the digital possibilities have presented us with a highly globalized world, objects have stayed at least partly local; they are manufactured somewhere, transported, marketed, and sold, and used elsewhere by someone other than their maker. Moreover, they are material and tangible to us here and now, and the vast majority of objects will outlast us, left on dumps for the slow decay of natural decomposing. Consider, for example, a computer or digital tablet. The object itself will outlast the software that gives us the possibility to use it, that is, the software will evolve and leave the outdated technological object useless. On the other hand, a material object is necessary for the software to be put into use. This line of thinking underlies the concept of media archae-

Claydies, Karin Kjældgård-Larsen and Tine Broksø, working blindfolded, 2011

ology, a nexus within media studies and history that examines how the evolution of physical objects—the media—from the wax plates of the Greeks to the electronic tablets of today, impacts functions and aesthetics and influences content and, finally, makes that content possible.

The objects of our time fascinate and annoy us because of their incapacity to remain up to date with the fast-paced evolution of the digital age, and the speed of mass production. In response, we are ever-more intrigued by handmade objects, most importantly those that are time-consuming to make and require the virtues of craftsmanship: highly developed skill, a certain amount of effort, and the desire to do the best possible work for its own sake.[5]

The consumer's shift in attention has not been ignored by companies that are trying to tap into their pockets—from those catering to the Do It Yourself (DIY) crowd, on the one hand, to designers, high-end galleries, and art fairs, on the other. When French luxury-goods firm Hermès organized the Festival des Métiers in New York in September 2012, inviting the company's artisans from the workshops in Paris and Lyon and installing them in a lavish studio space in a Park Avenue mansion,[6] the company clearly catered to the idea that quality equals handmade, and handmade equals exclusive. Craftsmanship and time-consuming work were on display when the artisans dyed silk scarfs and stitched leather bags while explaining the elaborate process for the audience. Judging from the amount of press coverage the event received, the idea of craftsmanship, manual labor, and luxury goods hit a soft spot. Bloggers and collectors alike marvel at the sight of the hard work and long process—two years for a silk scarf —which these sought-after objects entailed. One woman reportedly declared: "And to think I used to believe these scarves were expensive."[7]

Kim Joon
*Fragile-Dresden*, 2010 (detail)
Digital print

## PROCESS, MANUAL LABOR, AND MASS PRODUCTION

What the diverse craft-artists across the world today inevitably have in common is their bond to a certain material and the actual production of objects. The material is often the starting point of the artwork, that is, the underlying concepts are often derived from attributes specific to a material. Because of this, craft-artists have had a long and mutually beneficial tradition of collaborating with the craft industry: the ceramic and textile factories in Great Britain and Scandinavia are particularly good examples. However, as our profit-driven society no longer champions such production as economically feasible—unless it is outsourced to low-cost countries, out of sight and out of mind—what was once the industrial world has become a so-called postindustrial society, where we only design what will be laboriously produced elsewhere.[8]

The craft-artist is left behind as the sole agent of craftsmanship in the Northwestern hemisphere. This position is both challenging and crucial. Just as craft objects have been replaced by mass production, craft-artists are outsourcing the production of their work, a trend that raises ethical questions as well as questions of value and artistic status. Who is the artist? Is the craft-artist losing his craft, becoming "nothing but" an artist, creating concepts produced by craftsmen at a lower level of the hierarchy of production?

Small pottery production factory,
Jingdezhen, China, 2012

Many well-known artists and craft-artists benefit from the craftsmanship of others in their own work. Although there is and has been a strong tradition for craft-artists to lean on local skilled craftsmen for bigger projects, art objects are increasingly crafted in low-cost countries. The most interesting thing about this is not what is usually lamented—the fact that the artist does not craft the object himself, or possible exploitation of workers—but that the requisite craftsmanship in many cases has disappeared from Western countries, making it impossible to achieve the level of expertise necessary for the crafting of certain objects. The craftsmanship itself has been outsourced. Because of this outsourcing of production, the tools and equipment needed for certain artisanship are no longer available in the West. Craft artists no longer have access to ceramic or textile factories to make their art, because factories are being shut down or moved to lower-cost countries.

The downside of outsourcing for Northwestern craftsmanship is quite obvious, but from the global perspective of craft, outsourcing becomes more interesting. Northwestern craft artists most often are educated artists who traditionally have had creative and productive collaborations with specialized factories, the Scandinavian and British porcelain, glassware, and textile factories being exemplary examples. When the factories of these industries in recent years relocated to low-cost countries in Asia, not only did the collaborations with esteemed craft-artists come to a halt, the communities who based their livelihood on a certain set of skills were left without work. On the other hand, although outsourcing surely benefits some workers in low-cost countries, who may advance their skills, methodologies and designs, it also leads to widespread exploitation of workers, most clearly displayed in the devastating Rana Plaza factory collapse in Bangladesh of 2013. As such, the visibility of the work of craft-artists gains in importance, as it may function as a constant reminder of the ethical consequences of goods.

The Chinese artist Ai Weiwei is working on the threshold between art and craft, always relying on artisanship and craftsmanship in the production of his work, even if in most cases his art doesn't depend upon his own manual work, but rather is realized by a highly skilled and dedicated studio of collaborative craftsmen. Weiwei places importance on the work of craftsmen (and materiality alike), as he has said: "If we push the boundaries of craftsmanship and artisanship, we see that they are not just mechanical skills but are actually an exploration of the very nature of the materials they employ, a challenging, a questioning of wood or stone materials. This changes our perspective."[9] Questioning the nature of the materials utilized in making an object is at the core of Ai Weiwei's artistic practice as well as that of many other craft-artists today. This is what the diverse field of craft-artists worldwide has in common: an interest in and exploration of materials and materiality, on that account Ai Weiwei might be included in my definition of a craft-artist. Even where conceptual craft has taken a leading position in the craft field—for example, within ceramics and textiles in Britain and the Scandinavian countries—this exploration of materials is happening because to many craft artists in these countries, the material is the concept. Not only does the chosen medium influence how the message (the concept) is perceived, it also affects the very message itself. A symbiotic relationship occurs between the medium and the message, the material and the concept. Material is the starting point for any craft artist—in reality what separates a craft artist from artists in general—thus materiality becomes both the medium and the message.[10]

## FROM STONEWARE TO SOFTWARE

Media archaeology, which takes a material approach to media studies, may be a metaphor for what is happening within the crafts field. What craft-artists today are doing is a form of archaeological excavation of our contemporary society. In "Cultural Archive versus Technomathematical Storage," Media scholar Wolfgang Ernst writes about different types of memories in different media.[11] Ernst describes how media memory have shifted from the permanent, only readable memory of analogue or low-tech media, to the ever-changing and more dynamic memory of the new digital media. Likewise, many craft-artists today, especially those who work in ceramics and textiles, but equally with wood, leather and glass, transform their material from being exactly that—a material—and an object with a particular set of qualities, into a forceful device for creating connections and dialogue between present and past material practices. This dialogue can enable craft to function as a tool for appreciating the persisting hierarchies of values in the art world, and comprehending

how the market economy drives socio-economic development of mass production. Clare Twomey's *Made in China* (2011), eighty-one large, red urns, deals with exactly these issues. Only one of the urns was handmade. A factory in Asia produced the rest. While it took twenty-one days to mass-produce and decorate eighty urns, it took just as long to decorate one urn by hand at the Royal Crown Derby in England.

Neil Brownsword
*Wishing I Was Pretty*, 2001
Glazed earthenware, metal
15 x 12 x 10 in.

Today, through various storage solutions, information can be preserved even if the media, the materiality, is destroyed. However, craft-artists demonstrate how their materials contain information that cannot be read and understood without the object itself. We need access to a wooden sculpture in order to appreciate the craftsmanship involved in its production and the structure, shape, and beauty of the material. The materiality of the object cannot be translated into code. Digital media needs a certain type of software to function and this software is its context, both historical and present. Take ceramics as an example: Any urn is a medium, but exactly what it conveys changes with its context, whether it is seen as a container for wine, or for social, economic or aesthetic value. Do we have the necessary set of concepts and horizons of understanding to "read" ceramic objects? Do we have the necessary software?

Media archaeology digs into the development of the physical medium. In this context "software" is what allows the media to communicate with the consumer, to read its meaning. Lacking this metaphorical software might explain why the western consumer no longer relates to the process, context, and conditions concerning the production of the things with which we surround ourselves. By working with ceramics, wood, or textiles, craft-artists prompt contemporary consumers to examine how they view objects made from these materials. Their practice elicits questions of the value related to different materials used within the arts, a discussion that diverges from the somewhat outdated discourse on the value of ordinary manufactured objects as art, introduced by Marcel Duchamp with his *Fountain* in 1917.

Wolfgang Ernst points to a dichotomy between the digital archival practice of today, and the material accumulation of different places and times in traditional archives such as libraries and museums.[12] He argues that what will remain, at a time when the world is marked by the constant reorganizing flux of digitization, is a material resistance or even counter-practice to that distinctly immaterial world.[13] While Ernst is discussing traditional media versus digitization in regards to archival practices, his idea can be transferred to a more general examination of society, where contemporary craft may function as a material resistance at a time when materiality and craftsmanship are removed from our daily lives. Ceramic artist Neil Brownsword uses ceramic waste found in the debris of England's oldest ceramic production, the closed factory sites of Stoke-on-Trent, to produce work that deals not only with its own industrial history, but with the political conditions of production and waste.

Craft artists are not only excavating the history of their chosen material, they are exploring our understanding of the value of materials—and ultimately, things—today. In this way, craft artists adopt an archival position in a double sense: as a historically based material counter-practice and as a participant in vibrant exchanges today. This is apparent to a varying degree and in various forms in all craft practices, whether it is a studio potter or a more conceptually oriented craft-artist. In a society that has outsourced its industry, craft excavates the history of production.

## CRAFT AND ITS GLOCAL POTENTIAL

The tension between the global in the local and the local in the global is acknowledged with the label "glocal." The challenge is to understand how our everyday behavioral patterns influence others in different cultures, and vice versa: how actions far away might affect our own lives. Art has a potentially significant role in this regard, for making visible the technological, economic and political structures that control the consequences of our actions. Craft has a specific function in balancing glocal priorities, with its insistence on the material and on craft skills within a global market-driven economy that values profit over quality.

Yarn-bombed leg of statue by textile artist and knit graffiti founder Magda Sayeg, Paris, 2009

Glocalization, a concept introduced by economists in the 1980s, emphasized that products should be adapted for particular local markets, while acknowledging that such specification influences the global market, with new local consequences in other places. When industrial craft production is outsourced, the production is pulled out of its local market and moved to a place where residents might not be particularly interested in the object that is being produced, or, for that matter, be able to afford it. The worker has no relation to the object he produces, neither before nor after production. The screw of alienation in the production of goods is twisted another turn as a result of globalization. Craft may contribute to a critique of this development by establishing a glocal perspective.

I would argue that the continued advancement of society, and our understanding of that very advancement, in part depends on the craft artist's knowledge of materials and production processes. The corollary to the quest for technological progress seems to be the belief that all that is needed in this world are designers and entrepreneurs. Craft artists focus on materiality and tradition as opposed to technological breakthroughs. The insistence on the creative act as something that is based on a material reality, with a past and a present context, reminds us that all entrepreneurial, non-material work on design is built upon previous material (and non-material) work, and framed by the limits of the available technology.

## THE TIME OF THE OBJECT

In a lecture at the Venice Biennial in 2011, Jacques Rancière posed the same question with which I opened this essay: *In What Time Do We Live?* Rancière argued that the *state of things*, how things are, is always a *state of time*. His perspective encompassed the state of things in society at large: the historical evolution of political action and freedom, the present situation as well as future possibilities.[14] The state of craft is also a state of time, a time that is rapidly changing. And as the relationship between craft and production is constantly changing, craft itself is changing.

Events such as Hermès' Festival des Métiers help educate consumers about the quality of handmade objects. What separates this from what craft-artists are doing? Are they not both making craftsmanship and production visible? They certainly are, and for some, the Hermès demonstration may have been an eye-opener with regard to the production of any goods.

But if craftsmanship simply becomes a quality of luxury products, a category that all other products are excluded from, then it simply becomes another tool in the construction of social hierarchies.

Craft-artists are artists, not craftsmen. By making craft for art's sake, the craft-artist may escape the symbolic language of the brand system and hierarchies that companies such as Hermès are trying to promote. A craft-artist working in a world where production is no longer visible has immense potential. By relying on the openness of meaning that characterizes all art, and while assuming the fundamental position of making production as a category visible, craft-artists are free to question and mirror their own position both in the present and the past. The joining of art and craft, of meaning and material production occurs at a time and place where close contact with the production of goods is no longer part of our everyday life, in a society where most people cannot see the relationship between society at large and their individual actions. Craft artists are, by their nature, political in Jacques Rancière's notion of the word, in that they make visible the activity of production in "post-industrial" societies.[15]

As globalization, capitalism, and exploitation of resources are tightly linked, the accelerating exchange of information, money, and things have negative consequences, leading to environmental challenges and increasing economic difference between producers, consumers, and the owners of capital. By creating art that insists on its materiality, and thus making sure that the "software" necessary to read the things with which we surround ourselves persists, the craft artist does what we all should do: activate the global in the local, and the local in the global. The constant challenge is what it means to live in a time of the object, yet at a time when the world seems particularly and remarkably immaterial.

1. The "we" in this question is, of course, a reflection of this writer's "I," that is, a Northwestern privileged subject, speaking from within the system we know as liberal democratic capitalism. It is my belief, however, that the topics I deal with here concern many more.

2. Caroline Roux, "What is Craft"? Website of the Victoria and Albert Museum. www.vam.ac.uk/content/articles/w/what-is-craft/

3. Jacques Rancière, *Dissensus On Politics and Aesthetics* (London: Continuum, 2010), 36.

4. Three-quarters of a century has passed since Alan Turing published his article" On Computable Numbers, with an application to the Entscheidungsproblem, "*Proceedings of the London Mathematical Society, Series 2*, 42 (1936–7): 230–265. Errata appeared in Series 2, 43 (1937): 544–546. The first electronic general computer was unveiled 67 years ago and the public was allowed access to the World Wide Web more than twenty years ago. Our digital world is still young, but hardly new any more.

5. Sociologist Richard Sennett enumerates these three elements of craftsmanship as he writes extensively on craftsmanship and its changing role through time and space, in *The Craftsman* (New Haven: Yale University Press, 2008).

6. The Festival des Métiers tour later continued to venues in San Francisco and Houston.

7. Emma Allen, "Craft Fair on Park," *The New Yorker*, Jan. 14, 2013.

8. This is an intentionally hyperbolic description of Northwestern societies: traditional industries still employ many from their constituent populations, and as wage levels are adjusted, some industries are even moving back to their traditional home base. But the tendency toward moving manufacturing to lower-wage cultures is clear.

9. Statement used in installation graphics in the exhibition *Ai Weiwei According to What?* at the Hirshhorn Museum and Sculpture Garden, Washington, DC, Oct. 7, 2012–Feb. 24, 2013.

10. Media theoretician Marshall McLuhan famously coined the aphorism "The medium is the message," in *Understanding Media, the Extensions of Man* (Berkeley, CA and Hamburg, Germany: Gingko Press, 2003 [1964, NY: McGraw-Hill]).

11. Wolfgang Ernst: "Cultural Archive versus Technomathematical Storage," in *The Archive in Motion: New Conceptions of the Archive in Contemporary Thought and New Media Practices*, Eivind Røssaak, et al. (eds.) (Oslo: Novus Press, 2010).

12. Ernst uses the term 'heterotopia,' developed by Michel Foucault in the essay "Of Other Spaces." http://foucault.info/documents/heteroTopia/foucault.heteroTopia.en.html

13. Regarding the twenty-first century and its archival practice, Ernst writes: "What will retroactively remain are isolated islands of archival storage, heterotopias of "counter-spaces" as defined by Michel Foucault, monumental and material resistance against dynamic and permanent reorganization of binary data, counter-practices in this age of general digitization driven by economical force." Ernst (2010), 58.

14. Published as Jacques Rancière, "In What Time Do We Live?" in *The State of Things*, Office for Contemporary Art Norway, (London: Koenig Books, 2012), 9-38.

15. "The essential work of politics is the configuration of its own space. It is to make the world of its subjects and its operations seen. The essence of politics is the manifestation of dissensus as the presence of two worlds in one." Jacques Rancière in *Dissensus On Politics and Aesthetics* (London: Continuum, 2010), 37.

# CERAMICS

Mia Görranson
*Squares of Nature*, 2012 (detail)
Glazed porcelain

# ASGER JORN

1914–1973

Danish

The Royal Danish Academy of Fine Arts, School of Design, Copenhagen, Denmark, 1944

Vinthers Seminarium, Teacher Training College, Silkeborg, Denmark, 1935

Asger Jorn was a Danish artist known primarily for his paintings, writings, and participation in artist collectives of the 50s and 60s. Jorn found creative expression in many different media, including ceramics, made primarily in Albissola, Italy. He had no formal training when he first began to work with clay in Silkeborg in 1953. H

e soon felt that clay was his perfect medium; it stimulated his imagination and suggested endless possibilities. His collaboration with potter Knud Jensen provided surfaces for alteration and surface design. The applications on his ceramic forms relate directly to the paintings Jorn produced with childlike drawings of animals and figures. He continued to work in clay throughout his artistic career.

Asger Jorn was a leader of the European experimental art group CoBrA— an acronym for Copenhagen, Brussels, and Amsterdam, cities that were the homes of its founders. The group included the Belgian writer Christian Dotremont, and the Dutch painters Corneille, Constant, and Karel Appel. Influenced by the surrealist movement and the ideals of primitive and folk art, these artists aimed to produce a culturally specific Nordic expressionism. Jorn and the CoBrA group's work with clay represents a physical uprising against formalism and the Bauhaus movement. Jorn was not a household name in the United States because he avoided the NYC art scene, rejecting hierarchy and status in the arts, and refused several prestigious awards both in the United States and abroad. However, his work in ceramics had a profound influence during the twentieth century that persists in contemporary works.

Collections: Mildred Lane Kemper Art Museum, St. Louis, MO; Museum of Modern Art, NY; Stedelijk Museum, Amsterdam.

References: Michael Boylen, "The Ceramics of Asger Jorn," *The Studio Potter* 22, no. 12 (December 1993): 3.

Edmund de Waal, *20th Century Ceramics* (London and New York: Thames and Hudson, 2003), 140–142.

1

*Vessel*, 1953

Glazed ceramic

20¼ x 13 x 13 in.

Stéphane Janssen and R. Michael Johns Collection

# RUDY AUTIO

1926–2007

American

MFA, Washington State University, Pullman, 1952
BS, Montana State University, Bozeman, 1950

Rudy Autio was born in Butte, Montana, a booming copper mining town populated by diverse immigrant communities. Autio credits the local public school system and the WPA program with giving him his first exposure to the arts. After serving in the Navy for two years during WWII, Autio returned home and attended Montana State University on the GI Bill, where he studied ceramics under Frances Senska, and cemented a life-long friendship with Peter Voulkos, a fellow classmate. Autio served as Professor of Ceramics and Sculpture at the University of Montana in Missoula until he retired in 1985.

His early work, inspired by Voulkos and his work at Black Mountain College, was primarily gestural abstracted vessel forms. Today Autio is best remembered for his sculptural ceramics, altered vases rich with figurative drawings of women and horses, inspired by his childhood memories. He is referred to as the "Matisse of ceramics" for his use of vivid colors and masterful drawing techniques. [1] His legacy, in addition to his body of work, includes the numerous artists he taught and influenced as well as his role in establishing the Archie Bray Foundation while serving with Voulkos as its first co-director.

Collections: Metropolitan Museum of Art, NY; Los Angeles County Museum of Art; Carnegie Museum of Art, Pittsburgh.

References: Rudy Autio, interview by Lamar Harrington, Oct. 10, 1983 and Jan. 28, 1984, unpublished transcript, Archives of American Art, Smithsonian Institution.

1. Rick Newby, "Rudy Autio: Coming Home to the Figure," Rudy Autio: *The Infinite Figure*, exhibition catalogue (Helena: Holter Museum of Art, 2006), 6.

2

*Ceramic Pot,* 1966
Glazed stoneware, luster
16¼ x 12½ x 6½ in.

Purchased with funds provided by the
American Art Heritage Fund

# PETER VOULKOS

1924–2002

American

MFA, California College of the Arts, Oakland, 1952
BS, Montana State College, Bozeman, 1951

Over the course of a career spanning fifty years, Peter Voulkos had an
indelible impact on the world of ceramics. He was one of the founders of
the Archie Bray Foundation, organized and chaired two significant college
ceramic departments, led a revolution in the field of ceramics that spawned
a new generation of contemporary American ceramic artists, inspired
generations of students and artists, and produced a prolific body of work
that continues to set the standard for ceramics. After serving in the US Air
Force, Voulkos took advantage of the GI Bill to study painting and printmak-
ing at Montana State College in Bozeman, where he casually enrolled in a
ceramics class with Frances Senska and shifted his major from painting to
clay. After teaching a summer session at Black Mountain College, through
an invitation from Karen Karnes, Voulkos was introduced to John Cage, Josef
and Anni Albers, and more importantly, the ideology of abstract expressionism and the work of William de Kooning in New York City. This experience
forever changed the dynamics of his approach to clay. Subsequently, he
translated the methods of action and spontaneity that existed within the
abstract expressionist movement into the language of ceramics in his work.
His innovative methods of working in clay also provided new opportunities
for other clay artists to break through the rigid boundaries of craft and enter
the fine art world.

Voulkos received numerous awards over the course of his career, including the
Charles Fergus Binns Medal for Lifetime Achievement in Ceramic Art from
the New York State College of Ceramics at Alfred University; three National
Endowment for the Arts awards; a Guggenheim Foundation Award and the
Louise Nevelson Award from the American Academy and Institute of Arts
and Letters. Voulkos was also made an honorary member of the American
Academy and Institute of Arts and Letters in addition to his six honorary
doctorate degrees.

Collections: Brooklyn Museum, NY; Museum of Contemporary Art, Chicago;
Los Angeles County Museum of Art.

References: Ivy Barsky, "Peter Voulkos," *Philadelphia Museum of Art Bulletin* 87, no.
371/372 (Autumn 1991): 11.

Rose Slivka and Karen Tsujimoto, *The Art of Peter Voulkos* (Tokyo and Oakland, CA:
Kodansha International and the Oakland Museum of California, 1995).

3
*Steel Pot*, 1968
Glazed stoneware
32½ x 11½ x 11½ in.
Purchased with funds provided by the
American Art Heritage Fund

# MARILYN LEVINE

1935–2005

Canadian

MFA, University of California, Berkeley, 1971
MS, University of Alberta, Edmonton, Canada, 1959
BS, University of Alberta, Edmonton, Canada, 1957

Marilyn Levine was originally trained as a chemist before studying with Jack Surles in Saskatchewan. This early relationship with Surles lead to the development of a technical process utilizing fiberglass strands that achieved the maximum firing strength in clay. This process enabled endless possibilities with clay construction.

Levine found her signature style by translating everyday objects into sculptural works and became a virtuoso at the trompe-l'oeil technique. Her hyper-realistic renderings in clay of everyday leather objects have an attention to detail that capture both the history and humanity of the object. Her sculptures have been critically accepted in both the ceramics community as well as in the broader fine arts.

Collections: Los Angeles County Museum of Art; Everson Museum of Art, Syracuse, NY; Museum of Contemporary Art, Chicago.

References: Marilyn Levine, interview by Glenn Adamson, May 15, 2002, unpublished transcript, Archives of American Art, Smithsonian Institution.

Maija Bismanis, "Some Fragmented Thoughts About Clay," *Marilyn Levine: A Retrospective*, exhibition catalogue, (Saskatchewan: Mackenzie Art Gallery and The Canada Council for the Arts, 1998), 11–25.

4

*Dark Grey Satchel*, 1974
Earthenware, stains, luster
8⁵/₈ x 14½ x 7³/₈ in.
National Endowment for the Arts Matching
Funds Grant

5

*Eyelet Boots*, 1979
Earthenware, stains, leather laces
8¼ x 15¼ x 5 in.
Gift of Anne and Sam Davis

# BETTY WOODMAN

b. 1930

American

New York State College of Ceramics, Alfred University, 1948–1950

Betty Woodman began her career as a production potter, but her work has evolved to encompass a complex body of highly decorated ceramic sculpture. She made the shift from functional pottery to sculptural forms during the late 1970s while working primarily with earthenware. She is well known for her "Pillow" vessels, forms glazed with bright, saturated colors and painterly surface designs. Woodman made her first trip to Italy in 1951, working with Giorgio Ferrero. Italy opened her eyes to the wider field of ceramic art, and she was to fall in love with the vast possibilities of pottery as well as Italy itself. Woodman's work continued to evolve as she split her time between Colorada and Italy. She began to explore
salt firing, making large pots influenced by the Roman and Etruscan ceramic wares. Woodman's conceptual approach, paired with historical references and the ceramic medium, combine to form her signature sculptural style.

In 2006 she was honored as the first living woman artist to have a retrospective exhibition at the Metropolitan Museum of Art, NY. For almost twenty years, Woodman taught at the University of Colorado, Boulder, where she is now Professor Emeritus.

Collections: Museum of Arts and Design, NY; Detroit Institute of Arts; Victoria and Albert Museum, London.

References: Kelly Leigh Mitchell, "Betty Woodman," *Philadelphia Museum of Art Bulletin* 87, no. 371/372 (Autumn 1991): 36.

Grace Glueck, "Betty Woodman, Turning the Humble Vase into High Art," *New York Times*, http://www.nytimes.com/2006/04/28/arts/design/28wood.html. accessed. 8/7/2012,

6

*Persian Pillow Pitcher,* 1980
Glazed earthenware
16³/₄ x 21⁵/₈ x 12½ in.
Gift of Jay and Joyce Cooper

# ROBERT ARNESON

1930–1992

American

MFA, Mills College, Oakland, CA, 1958
BFA, California College of the Arts, Oakland, CA, 1954.

Robert Arneson began his ceramics career as a student of Antonio Prieto at Mills College in Oakland, where he developed the technical skills necessary to work as a professional potter. After a few short teaching stints, he accepted a full-time teaching position at the University of California at Davis in 1962, building one of the most important programs in the country. Given the charge of initiating the clay program, which would entail designing and building the TB9 facilities, he attracted a roster of notable students including Ron Nagle, David Gilhooly, Richard Shaw, Richard Notkin, and Peter Vanden-Berge. To dispel the notion of craft associated with the hobbyist, Arneson predicated his teachings on ceramics as a process within art pedagogy and avoided any association with the craft field.

Arneson returned to the kitsch notion of ceramics in his work of the 1960s, which took on a sociopolitical context and sculptural form. Arneson's "self-proclaimed marginalization" in ceramics led to the use of the term "funk" to identify his work. [1] The California funk movement of the 60s reflects humor in the work, with content at the forefront and forms and processes second. Arneson is best known for sculptural portraits of himself and other artists. Along with Viola Frey, Arneson is credited with the revival of the figure in the 1960s.

Collections: Hirshhorn Museum and Sculpture Garden, Washington, DC; Metropolitan Museum of Art, NY; Whitney Museum of American Art, NY.

Reference: Robert Arneson, interview by Madie Jones, Aug 14–15, 1981, unpublished transcript, Archives of American Art, Smithsonian Institution.

1. Glenn Adamson, *Thinking Through Craft* (Oxford and New York: Berg, 2007), 148.

7

*The Abstract Expressionist* (Jackson Pollack Relief), 1985
Glazed ceramic
34 x 26 x 10 in.
Stéphane Janssen and R. Michael Johns Collection
Art © Estate of Robert Arneson/Licensed by VAGA, New York

# BEATRICE WOOD

1893–1998

American

Académie Julian, Paris, 1910

Beatrice Wood was born in San Francisco and raised in New York City. She traveled the world studying painting, and then theater, in Paris, New York, and later, Montreal. Known as the "Mama of Dada," Wood met Marcel Duchamp in New York during the early years of the movement. They became intimately linked and remained friends throughout his life.

Beatrice Wood studied ceramics in Los Angeles with Glen Lukens, Gertrud and Otto Natzler, and later Vivika and Otto Heino. She moved to Ojai, California in 1947, where she established a home and studio, settling into the life of a potter. Her signature vessels and tall, complex, multivolumed chalices were glazed in shimmering, lustrous golds, pinks, greens, and bronzes. She also worked with more sculptural forms, coining the term "sophisticated primitives" for the child-like figures that referenced her love of folk art and certain elements of Dadaism. The last quarter century of Wood's life was her most prolific period of production. She had found her own voice, both in life and in art. She continued to write and make artwork until she died at 105 years old.

Collections: Crocker Museum of Art, Sacramento, CA; Metropolitan Museum of Art, NY; Museum of Fine Arts, Boston.

References: Beatrice Wood, interview by Paul Karlstrom, Aug. 26, 1976, unpublished transcript, Archives of American Art, Smithsonian Institution.

Beatrice Wood, interview by Paul Karlstrom, Mar. 2, 1992, unpublished transcript, Archives of American Art, Smithsonian Institution.

8

*Untitled Teapot,* 1987

Glazed stoneware

18 x 19 x 10 in.

Stéphane Janssen and R. Michael Johns Collection

# ARMAN (ARMAND FERNANDEZ)

1928–2005

American, born France

Ecole du Louvre, Paris, 1951
Ecole Nationale des Arts Décoratifs, Nice, France, 1949
BA, Philosophy and Mathematics, The Academy of France, Paris, 1946

The French artist Armand Pierre Fernandez, known as Arman, is widely recognized for his work with everyday objects and as a co-founder and member of Nouveau Réalisme. His 1955 neo-Dadaist works, which he called 'Cachets,' constructed from postal stamps and fabric scraps, were accumulated and assembled out of everyday objects; a technique inspired by the Dadaist collages of Kurt Schwitters. Being strongly influenced by Dada, his work, in turn, had a strong influence on pop art. Beginning in the mid-1960s, Arman made numerous visits to New York, acquiring American citizenship in 1972. The availability of mass-produced objects in the United States redirected his work toward new and more abstract accumulations. The process of accumulation, or, the layering of similar objects, changed the scope and meaning of his forms.

Collections: Metropolitan Museum of Art, NY; Tate Gallery, London; Centre Pompidou, Paris.

References: "Artist biography," Arman Studio, accessed August 14, 2012, http://www.armanstudio.com/arman-biography-1-eng.html.

Garth Clark, *Shards: Garth Clark on Ceramic Art* (New York: Ceramic Arts Foundation and Distributed Art Publications, 2003), 2.

9

*Demie Tasse*, 1990, 58/175
Glazed porcelain
Dimensions variable
Gift of the Helme Prinzen Estate

# AKIO TAKAMORI

b. 1950

Japanese, active in the United States

MFA, New York State College of Ceramics, Alfred University, 1978
BFA, Kansas City Art Institute, Kansas City, MO, 1976

Growing up in the small industrial town of Nobeoka, in postwar Japan, Akio Takamori was exposed to village life at the medical clinic his father oper-

ated. The individuals who came into the clinic represented the "fullness of humanity," a concept that would later appear in his work. An exhibition of contemporary Western art in 1971 exposed Takamori to the ceramic works of such artists as Richard Shaw and Peter Voulkos. He then serendipitously received an invitation from Ken Ferguson in 1974 to come to the United States and continued his education at the Kansas City Art Institute. Although Takamori returned to live in Japan for some time after completing his graduate degree, he ultimately settled in the United States, living and working in Seattle.

His breakthrough works were his "envelope vessels," depicting two-dimensional figures breaking the picture plane on the surface of volumetric forms. Takamori began the "envelope" series in 1981, inspired by the eighteenth-century Japanese printmaker Kitagawa Utamaro (1753–1806). Takamori has been recognized with numerous awards and fellowships during his substantial career, including the USA Ford Fellow, election to the American Craft Council College of Fellows, the Joan Mitchell Foundation Painters & Sculptors Grant, and the Visual Artists Fellowship Grant presented by the National Endowment for the Arts.

Collections: Ariana Museum, Geneva; Victoria & Albert Museum; The Museum of Contemporary Ceramic Art, Shigaraki, Japan; Museum of Art and Design, NY.

References: Peter Held, "Between Clouds of Memory," *Between Clouds of Memory: Akio Takamori, A Mid-career Survey,* ed. Peter Held (Tempe, AZ: Arizona State University Art Museum and Ceramics Research Center, 2005), 21.

*Akio Takamori: Ceramic Sculpture,* exhibition catalogue (New York: Garth Clark Gallery, 2000), 22–25.

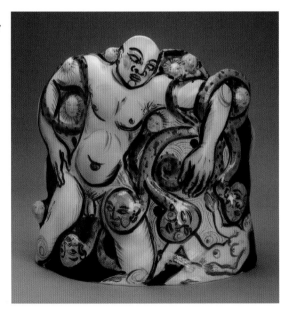

## 10

*Laocoön (Woman Reading),* 1994
Glazed porcelain, overglaze
25 x 21½ x 9 in.
Gift of Anne and Sam Davis

54

# VIOLA FREY

1933–2004

American

MFA, Tulane University, 1958

BFA, California College of the Arts (formerly CCAC), 1956

Viola Frey's early ceramic work reflects her interest in Japanese and Chinese ceramics of the twentieth century. The developments in contemporary ceramics and the new figurative painters working in San Francisco drew Frey back to the Bay Area in 1960 to further her work in clay. Viola was greatly influenced by the Funk ceramics of fellow California artist Robert Arneson and the paintings of Jean Dubuffet. She began to collect figurines and other small decorative works at flea markets, which she then incorporated into her large-scale sculpture. Frey's rural upbringing influenced her figurative subject matter: she models rural men and women with stiff poses and blank expressions.

Frey joined the faculty at CCAC in the early 1960s and remained a professor and chairman of the ceramics department there until her retirement in 1999. During her tenure she was instrumental in the design and building of the Noni Eccles Treadwell Ceramics Center on the Oakland campus of the college. In 2003 Frey was honored by the college with the establishment of the Viola Frey Chair in Fine Arts, which brings international ceramic artists as visiting professors and share their work with the Bay Area community. Her strong commitment to her work inspires generations of students, and her contribution to modern American ceramics has been profound.

Collections: Los Angeles County Museum of Art; Metropolitan Museum of Art, NY; Whitney Museum of American Art, NY.

References: Richard Whittaker, interviewer, "Who Makes Originals, Ever? A Conversation with Viola Frey," [*works + conversations*, no. 4 (February 2001): 10–19.

Viola Frey, interview by Paul Karlstrom, Feb. 27 and Jun. 19, 1995, unpublished transcript, Archives of American Art, Smithsonian Institution.

**11**

*Possessions I*, 1996

Glazed ceramic

23 x 25 x 18 in.

Gift of Sara and David Lieberman

# BETH CAVENER STICHTER

b. 1972

American

MFA, Ohio State University, Columbus, 2002
BA, Haverford College, PA, 1995

The connection between art and science has always been at the heart of the work of ceramic artist Beth Cavener Stichter. Her large-scale solid forms are constructed on steel armatures with wet clay, retaining the actions of the maker in gestural expressions. She selects a menagerie of goats, hares, and horses related to children's literature and fables as her subject matter. She believes that the emotions of all animals, both feral and domesticated, are shared at the most basic level. These emotions are depicted in human scale in her sculptural forms.

Stichter has been awarded artist-in-residence at several programs including the Archie Bray Foundation for the Ceramic Arts in Helena, Montana, and the Clay Studio in Philadelphia. She has also been the recipient of numerous fellowships and grants, including an Emerging Artist Award from the American Crafts Council, 2003; an Ohio Arts Council Individual Artist Fellowship, 2005; and the United States Artists Trust fellowship in 2009.

Collections: Chazen Museum of Art, Madison, WI; Contemporary Art Museum, Honolulu; Museum of Fine Arts, Houston.

References:  Liz Howe, "On Tender Hooks," *Ceramics Monthly* 58 (February 2010): 26–27.

Sheri Boggs, "Chris Antemann and Beth Cavener Stichter," *Ceramics: Art and Perception* 56 (June 2004): 23–27.

12
*Object Lesson: Apathy*, 2003
Stoneware, terra sigillata
27¼ x 30 x 22½ in.
Diane and Sandy Besser Collection

# TAKASHI HINODA

b. 1968

Japanese

BFA, Osaka University of Arts, Japan, 1991

Takashi Hinoda is a master of his material and brings biomorphic figurative forms to life. Hinoda is influenced by manga, anime, and American comics, and utilizes stylized surface designs that reference comics with their black outlines, bold colors, and matte finishes. His large-scale installations combine the two- and three-dimensional with sculptural forms and wall and floor graphics. Hinoda is Associate Professor of Ceramics at Kyoto Saga University of Arts in Japan.

Collections: Musée de la Ville de Vallauris, France; National Museum of Art, Osaka; Mint Museum of Craft+ Design, Charlotte, NC.

References: Naomi Tsukamoto, "Takashi Hinoda's Alternative Muscles," *Ceramics Monthly* 59, no. 8 (Aug. 2011): 36–39.

D.H. Rosen, "New Millennium Japanese Ceramics," *New Millennium Japanese Ceramics: Rejecting Labels and Embracing Clay*, exhibition catalogue (Minneapolis: The Northern Clay Center, 2011), 10–13.

13

*Everyday War,* 2004

Glazed ceramic

21⁵/₁₆ x 11¹³/₁₆ x 10³/₁₆ in.

Purchased with funds provided by the Herbert H. and Barbara C. Dow Foundation

# ANDERS RUHWALD

b. 1974

Danish

MFA, Royal College of Art, London, 2005
BA, The School of Design, Bornholm, Denmark, 2000

Anders Ruhwald investigates the relationships between sculpture, architecture, furniture, and ceramics in his body of work. He is keenly aware of the relationship between audience perception of object placement and their inter-relationships. Ruhwald approaches making from a formal standpoint that is involved in the reworking of an object in order to create a visual memory or a simulacra of an existing object.

He was awarded the Sotheby's Prize in the United Kingdom in 2007 and the Annie and Otto Detlefs Prize in Denmark in 2005. Currently, he is the Artist-in-Residence and Head of the Ceramics Department at Cranbrook Academy of Art.

Collections: Victoria and Albert Museum, London; Detroit Institute of Arts; National Museum of Decorative Arts, Trondheim, Norway.

References: Janet Abrams, "Object Relations," *Anders Ruhwald and Marie Torbensdatter Hermann,* exhibition catalogue (Glen Ellyn, IL: Gahlberg Gallery, College of DuPage, 2011), 6.

Sean Francis, "Anders Ruhwald," *Ceramics Monthly* 56, no. 6 (June 2008): 21–22.

**14**

*You Are Here, This Is It*, 2006

Glazed earthenware, painted steel, piping, rubber caps

20 x 18 x 21 in.

Gift of the Artist

**15**

*Form and Function, #2*, 2006

Glazed earthenware, painted steel, piping, rubber caps

30 x 40 x 28 in.

Purchased with funds provided by the Windgate Charitable Foundation

# LOUISE HINDSGAVL

b. 1973

Danish

MFA, Designskolen, Department of Ceramics and Glass, Kolding, 1999
Cencal, Caldas de Reina, School of Ceramics, Portugal, 1997

Louise Hindsgavl's ceramics career had a meteoric start upon her graduation in 1999. Her first exhibition featured figurative ceramic sculptures that derived more from kitsch than traditional art. Her work broke the boundaries of what was then the norm in Danish ceramics: the vessel as both subject and content. Hindsgavl plays on the tradition of porcelain figurines as depictions of innocent scenes, juxtaposing these white tableaux with mythical creatures that display overwhelming desires. The unsettling narrative content of her work, along with her interest in aspects of design, reveal her intention to reinterpret the figurative genre, as well as expand the audience's expectations of narrative ceramics.

Collections: Röhsska Museum Gothenburg, Sweden; National Museum of Decorative Arts, Trondheim, Norway; Danish Museums of Art & Design, Copenhagen and Trapholt.

Reference: Jorunn Veiteberg, "Louise Hindsgavl: Burleske Tableauer," *In Reality,* exhibition catalog (Copenhagen, Denmark: The Danish Arts and Crafts Association and the Danish Museum of Art and Design, 2006).

16
*The Required Action,* 2010
Glazed porcelain, mixed media
25 x 27 x 16 in.
Anonymous Gift

# STEEN IPSEN

b. 1966

Danish

MFA, The Royal Danish Academy of Fine Arts, School of Design, Copenhanmark, 1990

Steen Ipsen approaches clay through a combination of influences, including architecture, design, and materiality. Ipsen has a strong relationship with the geometrical universe, which he interprets in abstract sculptural form. He is a founding member of Copenhagen Ceramics, an exhibition platform that aims to showcase and demonstrate the high quality and great diversity of contemporary Danish ceramics. Ipsen also served as the head of the Institute of Glass and Ceramics at The Royal Danish Academy of Fine Arts, School of Design until 2004 and has been a member of the board of Danish Crafts at the Danish Ministry of Culture since 2006.

Collections: Victoria and Albert Museum, London; Icheon World Ceramic Center, Korea; Trapholt Art Museum, Kolding, Denmark.

Reference: Bent Lauridsen, *Steen Ipsen*, exhibition catalogue (Hong Kong: Galerie NeC Nilsson and Chiglien, 2012).

17

*Tied Up #62*, 2010

Glazed stoneware, cord

12 x 17½ x 10½ in.

Purchased with funds provided by the Windgate Charitable Foundation

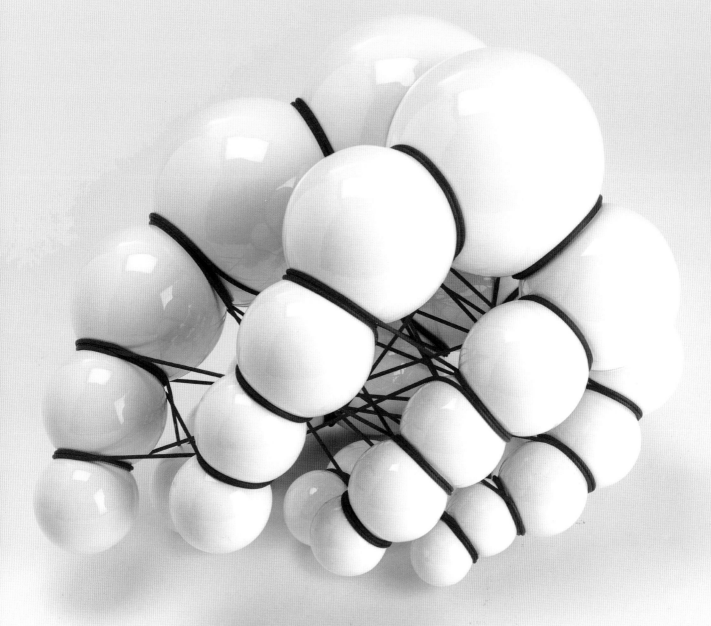

# LINDA SORMIN

b. 1971

Thailand, resides in Canada

MFA, New York State College of Ceramics, Alfred University, NY, 2003
BFA, Andrews University, Sheridan School of Craft & Design, Oakville, ON, 2001
BA, Andrews University, Berrien Springs, MI, 1993

Linda Sormin works in ceramics and mixed media, using objects and site-specific installations to explore issues of fragility and aggression, mobility and survival. Sormin collects and invites contributions of broken or discarded ceramic pieces to be included in her sculptural work. Born in Bangkok, Sormin earned a BA in English Literature and worked in community development for four years in Thailand and Laos, People's Democratic Republic. Many of her recent projects are site-specific and include the local community participation as part of her process.

She has taught ceramics at the university level since 2003, at the Emily Carr University of Art + Design in Vancouver, British Columbia, and the Rhode Island School of Design in Providence. Sormin is currently based in Toronto, Canada and is a professor and Head of Ceramics at the Sheridan School of Craft & Design.

Collections: Schein-Joseph Museum of Ceramic Art, Alfred, NY; World Ceramic Exposition, Gyeonggi Province, Korea.

References: Diane Sherlock and Nicole Burisch, "Linda Sormin, Cheh-ae Siah: Two Views," *Ceramics: Art and Perception* 67 (March–May 2007): 27–31.

*Roaming Tales: Linda Sormin,* exhibition catalogue (Surrey, British Columbia: TechLab, Surrey Art Gallery, 2007).

18

*Wanli*, 2010

Glazed earthenware, found objects (metal ship, porcelain shards from dish by Sanam Emami)

20 x 22 x 23 in.

Purchased with funds provided by the Windgate Charitable Foundation

# HUANG BINYAN

b. 1984

Chinese

China Central Academy of Fine Arts, Beijing, 2002
Wu Zuoren Academy of Fine Arts, Beijing, 2001

Huang Binyan utilizes the ceramic medium to express the duality of
an ancient Chinese past and a postmodernist aesthetic, representing
a rapidly changing contemporary urban life. Cartoons were first introduced to China from the West in the twentieth century; these references in her work signal her fascination with popular culture. Her subject
matter honors Chinese folk traditions while acknowledging influences
of western culture. Her work suggests the globalization of visual culture:
for example, Binyan's rabbit series references Jeff Koons' iconic Inflat-
able series of dogs, bunnies, and flowers. Both artists address such
social issues as consumerism and class roles within today's society.
Binyan is among the heirs of the seminal Chinese art movements of
political pop, kitsch, gaudy art and cynical realism.

**19**

*Rabbit #3*, 2011

Cast porcelain, overglaze

37½ x 12¾ x 9¾ in.

Gift of Anne and Sam Davis by exchange

# KAREN KJÆLDGÅRD-LARSEN

b.1974

Danish

MFA, Danish School of Design, Copenhagen, 2000

BFA, Danish School of Design, Copenhagen, 1998

# TINE BROKSØ

b.1971

Danish

MFA, Danish School of Design, Copenhagen, 2000

BFA, Danish School of Design, Copenhagen, 1998

Karen Kjældgård-Larsen and Tine Broksø, who function as the studio collective Claydies, met as fellow students at the Danish Design School in Copenhagen. Their partnership produces collaborations that are humorous, open-ended, and highly conceptual. The artists, who describe themselves as "one organism with two heads, two sets of imagination, four arms and four hands," run their design workshop in Copenhagen. The work of Claydies retains the inherent tactile qualities of clay while making a critical commentary on the current trend of removing all aspects of the handmade from clay as a counterpoint to form and concept. This approach explores and challenges ceramic history, resulting in the disintegration of previously held beliefs. Their work has been exhibited internationally in Europe and Japan.

Collections: Nationalmuseum, Stockholm, Sweden; Röhsska Museet, Gothenburg, Sweden; Malmö Konstmuseum, Sweden.

References: Rikke Helverskol Dahl, "CLAYDIES- A New Era For the Crafts?" *Claydies,* self-published catalogue, 2011, 14–16.

"Danish Crafts," *Crafts Collection* (January 2006): 14–16.

**20**

*True Feelings,* 2011

Glazed porcelain

Dimensions variable

Purchased with funds provided by the Windgate Charitable Foundation

# GUY MICHAEL DAVIS

b. 1979

American

MFA, Ohio State University, 2008
BFA, Kansas City Art Institute, 2003

# KATIE PARKER

b. 1980

American

MFA, Ohio State University, 2005
BFA, Kansas City Art Institute, 2003

Guy Michael Davis and Katie Parker collaborate as Future Retrieval. Both are ceramic and mixed media artists who utilize new technologies, including 3-D scanning, rapid prototyping, casting, and hand modeling. Conceptually, they are interested in ornamentation, detail, form, and natural order. The forms reference found objects, taxidermy, and museum collection objects or are directly assembled using these elements.

Their work has recently been exhibited at the Pennsylvania Academy of Fine Arts; the Fuller Craft Museum, MA; the Chelsea Art Museum, NY; and the Taft Museum, Cincinnati. Davis was awarded an artist-in-residency at the Walbzrych Porcelain Factory in Poland, 2011, where he worked with factory molds and decals to deconstruct patterns and forms. The collaboration received an emerging artist award from *Ceramics Monthly* that same year. Katie is an Assistant Professor at the University of Cincinnati, where Guy is a full-time Lecturer.

Collections: Society of Dresden Porcelain Art (Dresdner Porzellankunst e.V.), Frietal, Germany; Kansas City Art Institute, KS; The Pottery Workshop, Jingdezhen, China; Cincinnati Art Museum, OH

Reference: "Guy Michael Davis and Katie Parker, Emerging Artists, 2011," *Ceramics Monthly* 59, no. 5 (May 2011): 47.

21

*Hye-Que Monkey in Captivity,* 2011
Glazed porcelain, screenprint, wood
54 x 24 x 7 in.

Purchased with funds provided by the Windgate Charitable Foundation

# GUSTAF NORDENSKIÖLD

b. 1966

Swedish

MFA, Konstfack, Stockholm, 2001
BFA, University of Borås, Sweden, 1989

Gustaf Nordenskiöld combines elements of design, craft, art, and industrial production in his work. He uses the randomness of nature, the rawness of materials, and the mark of the tool to create everyday objects. His pieces have personal poetic value and raise questions about being and making. Capturing the memory of making in physical form is also an integral part of his practice.

Collections: National Museum, Stockholm; Röhsska Museet, Gothenburg, Sweden; Malmö Konstmuseum, Sweden.

22

*Mure*, 2011
Colored porcelain, rope
12 x 17½ x 10½ in.
Purchased with funds provided by the Windgate Charitable Foundation

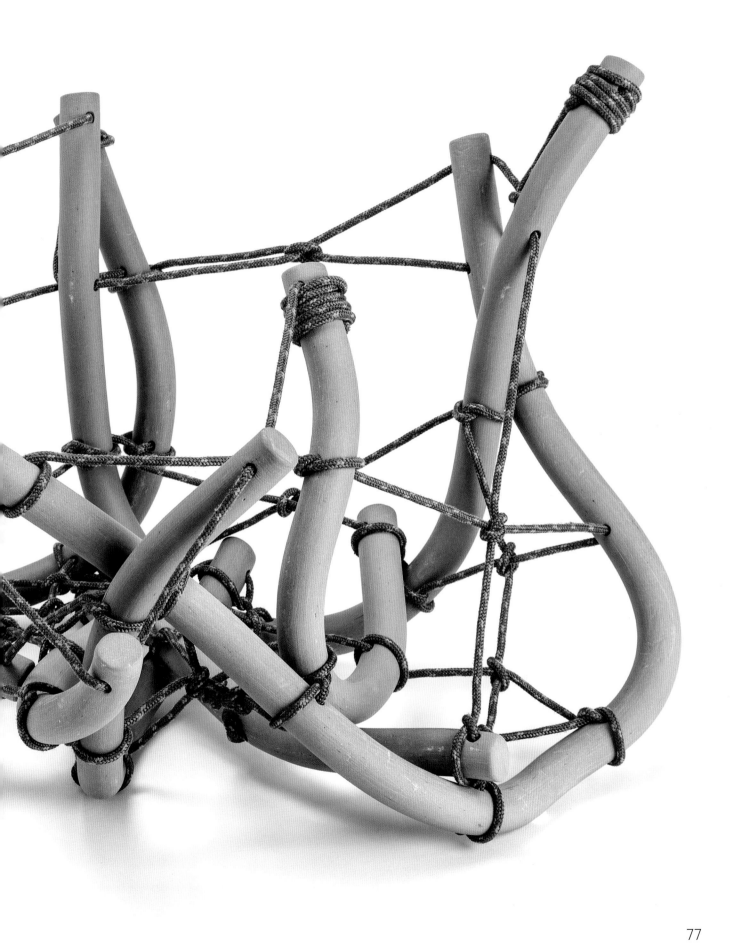

# PAUL SCOTT

b. 1953

British

PhD, Manchester Institute for Research and Innovation in Art and Design, Manchester Metropolitan University, Manchester, England 2010
BEd, Saint Martin's College, Lancaster, England, 1977
Certificate of Education, Saint Martin's College, Lancaster, England, 1975

Paul Scott is an artist, writer, and educator best known for innovative research that addresses the graphic nature of ceramic surfaces. His practice is based in the historical investigation of mass-produced tableware decorated with landscape patterns. Scott has developed new techniques for transfer prints, which were traditionally used to decorate industrially made dinner services. He creates ceramic landscapes that evoke an ideal pastoral landscape in the characteristic blue-and-white decoration of historical Chinese porcelain wares but on closer inspection, more sinister aspects of modern life subvert the bucolic in his designs. He was recently appointed Professor of Ceramics at the National Academy of the Arts, Oslo, Norway.

Collections: Victoria and Albert Museum, London; Danish Arts Foundation, Copenhagen; Museum of Arts and Design, NY.

References: Edmund De Waal and Claudia Clare, "Paul Scott," *The Pot Book* (London and New York: Phaidon, 2011), 243.

Amy Gogarty, "Paul Scott's Confected Landscapes and Contemporary Vignettes," *Ceramics: Art and Perception* 75 (March–May 2009): 51–56.

23
*Scott's Cumbrian Blue(s)- A Willow for Ai Weiwei, Wen Tao, Liu Zhenggang, Zhang Jinsong, Hu Mingfen*, 2011
Found object (porcelain, c. 1840), decals
8 11/16 x 10 5/8 x 1 3/16 in.
Gift of the artist

# PER B. SUNDBERG

b. 1964

Swedish

MFA, Konstfack College of Arts, Crafts, and Design, Stockholm, 1990

Per B. Sundberg began his artistic career as a ceramics student at Capellagården in Sweden. His work is a range of new interpretations of the traditional, mass-produced ceramic figurine. Sundberg has amassed a collection of more than 2,000 figurines, some of which he repurposes in a nod to Levi-Strauss and the ideas of bricolage. His execution is "brutal, and yet romantic, [made up of] still-lifes and objects."[1] His work has also been credited as being central to the spirited Swedish crafts movement of recent years.

Collections: Victoria and Albert Museum, London; Musée des Art Décoratifs de Montréal; National Museum, Stockholm.

Reference: 1. Maj Sandell, and Agneta Linton, "Foreword: Per Sunberg," exhibition catalogue (Gustavsberg, Sweden: Gustavsberg Konsthall, 2011), 16.

24

*The Gathering*, 2011

Glazed porcelain, found objects

11 x 9 x 9 in.

Purchased with funds provided by the Windgate Charitable Foundation

# ANDREW CASTO

b. 1977

American

MFA, University of Iowa, Iowa City, 2010

MA, University of Iowa, Iowa City, 2009

BA, Earlham College, Richmond, IN, 2000

Andrew Casto approaches his studio practice through personal examination of formal relationships to objects, and how gravity impacts these forms. Through multiple firings, his sculpture accumulates layers of slip, texture, glaze, and luster, resulting in eroded and geologic hybrids. His ceramics, combined with other media, result in visually arresting forms and textures that are both familiar and unknown.

Born in Delaware, Ohio, Casto returned to the Midwest as an Assistant Professor of Art at Mount Mercy University in Cedar Rapids, Iowa. He has served as an adjunct Assistant Professor at Augustana College in Illinois, Knox College in Illinois, and the University of Iowa.

He received the 2011–2012 Archie Bray Foundation's MJD Fellowship and the FuLe Prize, awarded by the International Ceramic Magazine Editors Association in Fuping, China.

Collections: Archie Bray Foundation for the Ceramic Arts, Helena, MT; Centre Culturel d'Andenne, International Ceramics Permanent Collection, Andenne, Belgium; Maruchu Gallery, Toki City, Japan.

25

*Assemblage 44*, 2012

Glazed ceramic, gold luster, paint, wood, metal

71¾ x 66 x 31 in.

Purchased with funds provided by the Windgate Charitable Foundation

# MIA E GÖRANSSON

b. 1961

Swedish

MFA, University College of Art Crafts and Design, Stockholm, 1994

BFA, Hovedskous School of Art, Gothenburg, 1987

Born in Stockholm, the younger of two daughters, Göransson grew up in Linköping, the center of the Swedish aircraft industry and cutting-edge technology. Her father's interest in botany immersed her in plant life and nature at an early age. When she was 19, she took a job at a pottery in Visby where she learned the fundamentals of ceramics.

Detail and the precision of craft skill are characteristic of Göransson's work. She is informed by the history of clay infused with modern design sensibilities. She is able to capture nature in its genesis, capturing the germination of plants often associated with spring. Göransson casts dark terracotta clay with pure white glaze and arranges the individual objects into installations and still-lifes. Göransson is visiting professor at HDK, School of Design and Crafts in Gothenburg.

Collections: Röhsska Museum, Gothenburg, Sweden; Malmö Konstmuseum, Sweden; Museum fur Kunst und Gewerbe, Hamburg, Germany.

Reference: Petter Eklund, "Portrait," *Mia E Göransson,* exhibition catalogue (Gustavsberg: Gustavsberg Konsthall, 2010), 10–18.

26

*Squares of Nature,* 2012

Glazed porcelain

36 x 36 x 3 in.

Purchased with funds provided by the Windgate Charitable Foundation

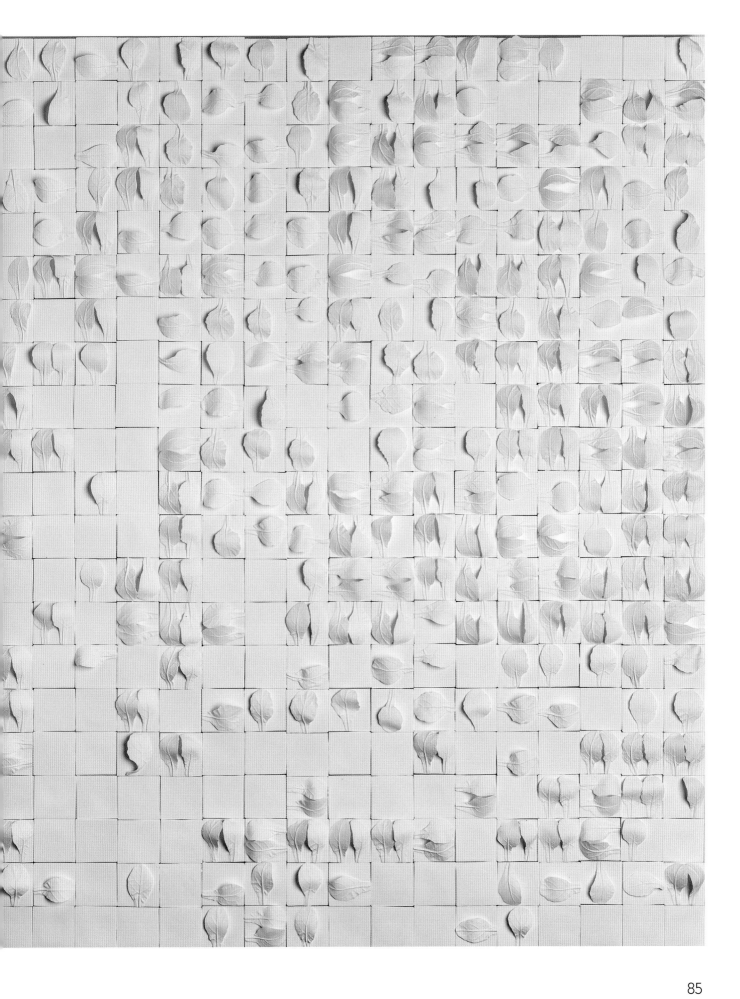

# DEL HARROW

b. 1977

American

MFA, New York State College of Ceramics, Alfred University, 2005
BS, University of Oregon, Eugene, 1999

Del Harrow is a sculptor who employs digital fabrication to create
3-D models of abstract forms, then experiments with the placement,
arrangement, and organization of objects in installations. His work
explores the intersection of digital design and manual and skill-based
fabrication processes.

Harrow is an Assistant Professor of Art at Colorado State University in
Fort Collins. He previously taught at Penn State University and Kansas
City Art Institute.

Collections: Archie Bray Foundation for the Ceramic Arts, Helena, MT; Contemporary Craft Museum, Portland, OR; Nanfeng Foshan International Ceramics
Museum, China.

Reference: Iunia Ratiu and Vasi Hirdo, "Interview with Del Harrow, Exhibiting Artist
at the Overthrown: Clay Without Limits Exhibition, Denver Art Museum, July 2011,"
*Ceramics Now* (July 2011), http://www.ceramicsnow.orgpost/7896159959/inter-
view-with-del-harrow-exhbiting-artist-overthrown. Accessed November 28, 2012..

27

*Cabinet #3*, 2012

Porcelain, luster, wood

30 x 60 x 24 in.

Purchased with funds provided by the
Windgate Charitable Foundation

# DAVID HICKS

b. 1977

American

MFA, New York State College of Ceramics, Alfred University, 2006
BFA, California State University, Long Beach, 2003

Growing up amid the farmlands of Valencia, California, David Hicks developed an early interest in agriculture that continues to inform his creative process. His sculptures retain the qualities of organic forms common to the American landscape. Specifically, his work references agricultural cycles as symbolic of the human struggle: fertilization, growth, decay. He has recently begun exploring forms that reference botanical structures of plants and other vegetation.

Collections: World Ceramic Exhibition Foundation, South Korea; United States Embassy Art Collection; American Museum of Ceramic Art, Pomona, CA.

Reference: "Emerging Artists 2010: David Hicks," *Ceramics Monthly* 58 (May 2010): 60.

28
*Flora* (yellow melt), 2012
Glazed terracotta
24 x 15 x 14 in.
Gift of the Artist

# KARIN KARINSON NILSSON

b. 1970

Swedish

MFA, University of Gothenburg: HDK School of Design and Crafts, Sweden, 2011

BFA, Capellagården School of Craft and Design, Sweden, 2008

As a child, Karin Karinson Nilsson became obsessed with knickknacks, and fell in love with all things pink, shiny, and glittery. These treasures led her to a dreamland where anything could happen and the boundaries were set only by her imagination. Nilsson combines glass, clay, and readymades to create her fluid sculptures. She represents a younger generation of practitioners in the ceramics field who examine the properties of clay and glaze, pushing these materials to the limits of conventional practice.

29

*This Was Not a Sneak Attack*, 2012

Glazed porcelain, glass, mixed media

13 x 13½ x 10½ in.

Purchased with funds provided by the Windgate Charitable Foundation

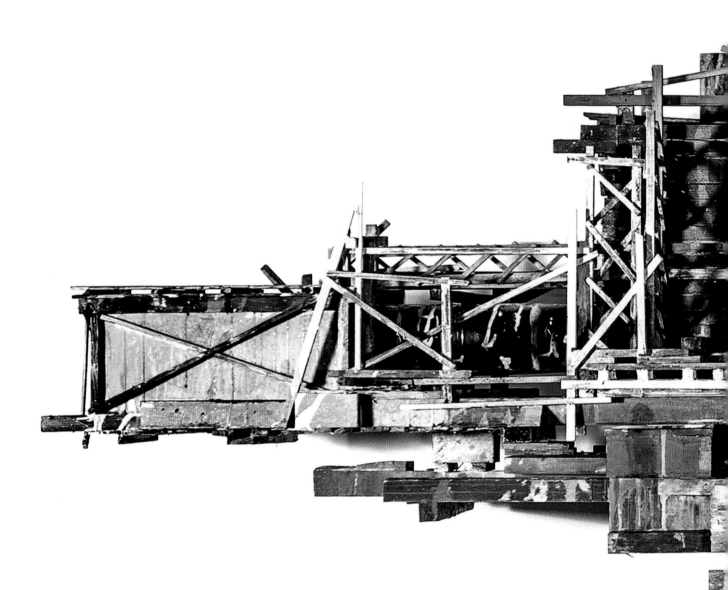

David Rowe
Untitled, 2011 (detail)
Recycled wood, mixed media

WOOD

# TOM ECKERT

b. 1942

American

MFA, Arizona State University, Tempe, 1971
BFA, Arizona State University, Tempe, 1966

Tom Eckert uses a wide variety of woodworking techniques, including lamination, bending, carving, and turning in his sculptural pieces. His nearly thirty years of experience as a professor and department head in the wood program at Arizona State University have brought personal insight to the techniques and materials he uses. Because of his superb skill, his trompe l'oeil objects transcend the natural qualities of wood.

Eckert has received two Visual Arts Fellowships from the Arizona Commission on the Arts and was awarded WESTAF/NEA grants in 1989 and 1993.

Collections: Racine Art Museum, WI; Los Angeles County Museum of Art; Museum of Arts and Design, NY.

Selected reference: Tom Eckert, Interview by Jo Lauria, June 19, 2007, unpublished transcript, Archives of American Art, Smithsonian Institution.

30

*MM 342 (Tank Chair)*, 1980
Hard maple
34½ x 30½ x 36 in.
Gift of E. Tom and Erika Meyer

# MARK LINDQUIST

b. 1949

American

MFA, Florida State University, Tallahassee, 1990
BA, New England College, Henniker, NH, 1971

At age 10, Mark Lindquist began to learn the traditional techniques of woodturning from his father, the well-known turner Melvin Lindquist. Mark creates dramatic and monumental sculptural forms and embraces the idea of "Happy Accidents," in which spalting, natural rims, holes, and cracks animate the works. Mark is credited with reviving the woodturning program at Haystack Mountain School of Crafts during the summer of 1979. Two years later, with the assistance of his father, the Lindquists started a woodturning program at Arrowmont School of Arts and Crafts in Gatlinburg, Tennessee.

In 1995, a twenty-five-year retrospective, *Mark Lindquist: Revolutions in Wood*, opened at the Hand Workshop Art Center in Richmond, Virginia. Lindquist is the 2010 recipient of the American Association of Woodturner's Lifetime Achievement Award.

Collections: Art Institute of Chicago; Museum of Fine Arts, Houston; Metropolitan Museum of Art, NY.

Reference: Robert Hobbs, *Mark Lindquist: Revolutions in Wood* (Richmond and Seattle: Hand Workshop Art Center and University of Washington Press, 1995).

31
*Unsung Bowl #1*, 1981
Cherry burl
9¾ x 10¹¹/₁₆ x 10¹¹/₁₆ in.
Gift of Edward Jacobson

# DAVID ELLSWORTH

b. 1944

American

MFA, University of Colorado, Boulder, 1973
BFA, University of Colorado, Boulder, 1971

David Ellsworth developed an interest in woodworking from an early age. He began constructing objects from materials his father cast off while building a cabin in the mountains of Colorado. When he graduated from college, Ellsworth was hired by ceramist Paul Soldner to be the woodworker-in-residence at Anderson Ranch in Snowmass, Colorado, where he developed the largely self-taught skills needed for furniture design and construction. This experience shaped his commitment to wood as a medium and to being an artist and educator. By the mid-1970s, he had developed a personal woodturning aesthetic and created a series of tools that produced thin-walled hollow forms. Ellsworth pushes the limits of his techniques by exploring concepts that move beyond the ideas inherent in beauty and the vessel. He is a founding and lifetime member of the American Association of Woodturners.

Collections: Philadelphia Art Museum; Museum of Fine Arts, Boston; Museum of Arts and Design, NY.

References: Mary Cheek Mills, "Artist Biography: David Ellsworth," in *Wood Turning in North America Since 1930* (Philadelphia and New Haven: Wood Turning Center and Yale University Art Gallery, 2001), 166.

Connie Mississippi, "Interview with David Ellsworth," *Collectors of Wood Art (CWA) Newsletter* (August 2007).

32
*Emerald Moon*, 1982
Lignum vitae
9½ x 7¼ x 7¼ in.
Gift of Edward Jacobson

# STEPHEN HOGBIN

b. 1942

British, resides in Ontario, Canada

MFA, Royal College of Art, London, 1965

BFA, Kingston College of Art, London, 1961

Stephen Hogbin is recognized internationally by collectors, educators, and professional organizations for his influence in studio woodturning. Since the early 1970s, he has developed a rich vocabulary of innovative, lathe-turned forms. He also works in bronze and stone, and has produced both large installations and small vessels. Primarily a studio artist with an inclusive and multidisciplinary approach, he also works as a curator and author.

Collections: Canadian Guild of Crafts, Toronto; Crafts Association of Victoria, Australia; Melbourne State College, Australia.

Reference: Edward Jacobson, *The Art of Turned-wood Bowls* (New York: E.P. Dutton, 1985), 29.

33

*Walking Bowl*, 1983

Zebrawood

10⅞ x 6⅞ x 8¼ in.

Gift of Edward Jacobson

# ED MOULTHROP

1916–2003

American

MFA, Princeton University, NJ, 1941.
BA, Case Western Reserve University, Cleveland, OH, 1939.

Ed Moulthrop is widely known as the "father of modern woodturning." Although he studied architecture and focused on this practice in his early professional career, Moulthrop decided to pursue woodturning professionally in the 1970s. He was most famous for his large-scale turned bowls made from domestic woods with polished, clear finishes. He designed and built the majority of his equipment and developed his own finishing process. Moulthrop was honored as a fellow of the American Craft Council in 1987.

Collections: Metropolitan Museum of Art, NY; White House Collection of American Crafts, Washington, DC; Museum of Arts and Design, NY.

References: Edward Jacobson, *The Art of Turned-wood Bowls* (New York: E.P. jj,,Dutton, 1985), 53.

Kevin Wallace, *Moulthrop: A Legacy in Wood* (Louisville, KY: Crescent Hill Books, 2007).

**34**

*Vessel*, 1990
Cedar
25 3/8 x 19 x 19 in.
Gift of the artist and The Hand and The Spirit

# VIRGINIA DOTSON

b. 1943

American

BFA, Arizona State University, Tempe, 1985

The Arizona landscape, where she resides and works in Scottsdale, is a major source of inspiration for Virginia Dotson. Born into a family of musicians, she translates the harmonies and rhythms of music into her wood vessels. Laminated wood blocks are lathe-turned then carved to create negative space within her vessel forms. Dotson describes her process as a combination of prehistoric technology and contemporary chemistry guided by the inherent character of natural wood.[1]

Collections: Smithsonian American Art Museum, Washington, DC; Los Angeles County Museum of Art; Contemporary Art Museum, Honolulu.

References: *Turned Wood Now: Redefining the Lathe-Turned Object IV* (Tempe, AZ: Arizona State University Art Museum, 1997), 13-14.

1. "Ask the Artist: Virginia Dotson," *The White House Collection of American Crafts,* http://americanart.si.edu/dotson.html (accessed October 15, 2012).

35
*Wind Eye Series,* #1, 1992
Marfim plywood, plexiglas
12¼ x 8½ x 8½ in.
Gift of the Artist

# PHILIP MOULTHROP

b. 1947

American

JD, Woodrow Wilson College of Law, Atlanta, GA, 1978
BA, West Georgia College, Carrollton, GA, 1969

Philip Moulthrop began his education in turning with his father, Ed
Moulthrop. He is the second in three generations of Moutlhrop woodturners. Philip lives and works in Marietta, Georgia, where he has been
refining his craft for more than thirty years. He was presented with the
Georgia Governor's Award for the Arts and Humanities in 2012 and is
widely recognized for his inlaid mosaic bowls made of Southeastern
indigenous woods.

Collections: High Museum of Art, Atlanta; Fine Arts Museum of the South, Mobile,
AL; Kresge Art Museum, East Lansing, MI.

Reference: Edward Jacobson, *The Art of Turned-wood Bowls* (New York:
E.P. Dutton, 1985), 57.

36

*White Pine Mosaic Bowl*, 1992

White pine, epoxy

15⁷/₈ x 18 x 18 in.

**Purchased with funds provided by the
American Art Heritage Fund**

# TODD HOYER

b. 1952

American

BA, Arizona State University, Tempe, 1975

Todd Hoyer learned the basics of woodturning during junior high in Phoenix, Arizona, later studying drafting before returning to wood-turning in the early 1980s. His background in drafting is evident in the geometric patterning of his sculptures and vessels, created by burning, cutting, and wrapping his works in rusted wire. Hoyer favors weathered and local woods found near his home in Bisbee, Arizona, such as cottonwood, elm, and palm. Hoyer has been called the "autobiographical turner" and his works have a raw, emotional quality inspired by personal emotions and experiences.

Collections: Smithsonian American Art Museum, Washington, DC; Detroit Institute of Arts; Yale University Art Gallery, New Haven, CT.

References: Nicholas R. Bell, *A Revolution in Wood: The Bresler Collection* (Washington, D.C: Smithsonian American Art Museum, 2011), 68.

*Turned Wood Now: Redefining the Lathe-Turned Object IV* (Tempe, AZ: Arizona State University Art Museum, 1997), 16.

37

*Ringed Series*, 1997

Cottonwood, wire

9 x 15 x 15 in.

Gift of Sara and David Lieberman

# CONNIE MISSISSIPPI

b. 1941

American

MFA, Pratt Institute, Brooklyn, NY, 1972

BFA, Memphis College of Arts, TN, 1963

Connie Mississippi was born and raised in the Mississippi Delta, where she was shaped as both a person and an artist. She found beauty in simple things and discovered her natural abilities as an artist while she was still a child. After she moved to Los Angeles, Mississippi painted on shaped three-dimensional canvases until she realized that she was actually making painted sculptures. She became interested in the lathe as a means for making sculpture and spent a year in 1983 working with Howard Lewin, a lathe artist. To celebrate her fiftieth year, she had fifty turned pieces hung in the Fig Gallery in Santa Monica.

Collections: Los Angeles County Museum of Art; Detroit Institute of Arts; Rockefeller University, NY.

Reference: Mary Cheek Mills, "Artist Biography: Connie Mississippi," in *Wood Turning in North America Since 1930* (Philadelphia and New Haven: Wood Turning Center and Yale University Art Gallery, 2003), 172.

38

*Evening Stillness*, 2000

Laminated Baltic birch plywood, paint

8 x 22 x 22 in.

Gift of Robyn and John Horn

# ROBYN HORN

b.1951

American

BA, Hendrix College, Conway, Arkansas, 1973

Robyn Horn was born in Ft. Smith, Arkansas, and worked in typesetting, photography, and stained glass, before she discovered woodworking. In 1984 she began turning bowls and vases on the lathe, moving later into more sculptural forms. Horn has always worked in a serial fashion, making sculptures with qualities of asymmetry, geometry, volume, contrast, and heavy textures. Horn, who lives and works in Little Rock, helped organize the Collectors of Wood Art (CWA), founded in 1997.

Collections: Crystal Bridges Museum of American Art, Bentonville, AR; Los Angeles County Museum of Art; Museum of Arts and Design, NY; Ogden Museum of Southern Art, New Orleans, LA.

Reference: Elisabeth Sövik, ed., *Conversations With Wood: The Collection of Ruth and David Waterbury* (Minneapolis: Minneapolis Institute of Arts, 2011), 109–114.

39
*Token Stone* from the *Slipping Stone Series*, 2003
Red gum burl
16½ x 18 x 6 in.

Purchased with funds provided by the Herbert H. and Barbara C. Dow Foundation

# HOWARD WERNER

b. 1951

American

BFA, Rochester Institute of Technology, NY, 1977

Howard Werner studied woodworking and furniture design and uses elements from functional objects in his sculptural forms. His greatest inspiration, however, draws from the world of sculpture, the work of Brancusi and Noguchi, classical forms from Greece and Italy, and African sculpture.

Werner has been direct-carving sculpture and furniture from large tree sections since the mid-1970s. His process is evident in the rough chainsaw surfaces and the untouched natural sections of the trees that are prominent in many of his works.

Collections: Museum of Arts and Design, NY; Arkansas Art Center, Little Rock; Rochester Institute of Technology, NY.

Reference: *Expressions in Wood: Masterworks From The Wornick Collection* (Oakland: Oakland Museum of California, 1996), 154–155.

40
*Poplar Vessel*, 2003
Poplar
56 x 38½ x 15¼ in.

Museum Purchase with funds provided by the Windgate Charitable Foundation

# CLAUDETTE SCHREUDERS

b. 1973

South African

MFA, University of Cape Town, South Africa, 1998
BA, University of Stellenbosch, South Africa, 1994

Claudette Schreuders creates hand-carved and painted wooden figures. These sculptures, many of them depicting women, strive to reflect the uncertainties encountered in the search for a contemporary African identity. Her work is influenced by the traditional figurative art of the Baule people of West Africa, as well as characteristics from medieval church ornamentation, Spanish portraiture, and Egyptian woodcarving. She chooses to show small bodies of work as sculptural installations in order to emphasize the narrative qualities of her work.

Collections: Pretoria Art Museum, South Africa; Metropolitan Museum of Art, NY; Museum of Modern Art, NY.

References: *The Long Day: Sculpture by Claudette Schreuders,* exhibition catalogue (Tempe, AZ: Arizona State University Art Museum, 2004).

Roberta Smith, "Claudette Schreuders," *New York Times,* December 6, 2002, E40.

41

*New Shoes,* 2003–2004
Jacaranda wood, enamel paint
30½ x 12 x 9¾ in.
Museum purchase with funds provided by th
Windgate Charitable Foundation

# EFRAIN ALMEIDA

b. 1964

Brazilian

Efrain Almeida uses cedar to create hand-carved sculptures that are rooted in the traditional folk objects made by craftsmen in northeastern Brazil. These sculptures appear crude and nostalgic, mimicking Brazilian folk art. Almeida's practice taps into the sacred and popular statuary used in the religious festivals of the sertão highlands in northern Brazil. He intertwines both traditional and personal iconographies with critical references to present-day culture. In this approach, his work takes on and explores stereotypical tropes of authenticity associated with folk traditions from Brazil.

Collections: Museu de Arte Moderna de São Paulo, Brazil; Centro Galego de Arte Contemporánea, Santiago de Compostela, Spain; Museum of Modern Art, NY.

Reference: Alexandre Melo, "Efrain Almeida," *Artforum International* 39, no. 5 (January 2001): 144.

42

Untitled, 2004

Cedar, plastic beads

60 x 48 x 5 in.

Purchased with funds provided by the Wind-gate Charitable Foundation

# YOSHIMASA TSUCHIYA

b. 1977

Japanese

PhD, Tokyo National University of Fine Arts and Music, Japan, 2007
MA, Tokyo National University of Fine Arts and Music, Japan, 2003
BFA, Tokyo National University of Fine Arts and Music, Japan, 2001

Yoshimasa Tsuchiya earned a doctorate in Conservation Studies with an emphasis on restoration of Buddhist images, training that informs his highly technical execution of carved wooden sculptures. He uses these traditional Japanese carving techniques to retain the authentic beauty and essence of the trees from which he constructs his mythological creatures. His concepts and motifs are inspired by Japanese folklore, myths, and his own dreams. To him, mythology is a series of allegorical stories passed on from generation to generation that maintains the identity of a group of people. His works are a balance of fancy and fright, and reference the popular anime and manga of Japanese culture.

Reference: Toshiaki Hozumi, "Yoshimasa Tsuchiya—The Very Reasons Why in a World of Silence," *Sylvan Whispers*, exhibition catalogue (Tokyo: Kyuryudo Art Publishing and Megumi Ogita Gallery, 2012), 77.

43

*Carnival,* 2005

Hinoki (Japanese cypress), paint, crystals

6 x 11 x 8 in.

Purchased with funds provided by the
Windgate Charitable Foundation

# ALISON ELIZABETH TAYLOR

b. 1973

American

MFA, Columbia University, NY, 2005

BFA, Art Center College of Design, Pasadena, CA, 2001

Alison Elizabeth Taylor grew up in Las Vegas, Nevada, and currently lives and works in Brooklyn, New York. Initially a painter, Taylor mastered the skill of marquetry shortly after her discovery of the Studiolo from the Ducal Palace in Gubbio, a spectacular use of marquetry for a decorative and narrative program, during a visit to the Metropolitan Museum of Art in 2003. Taylor pairs this traditional craft with socially conscious imagery in her work. She has been awarded the prestigious Louis Comfort Tiffany Award, as well as the Smithsonian Artist Research Fellowship, both in 2009.

Collections: Crystal Bridges Museum of American Art, Bentonville, AR; Des Moines Art Center, IA.

Reference: *American Gothic: Aaron Spangler & Alison Elizabeth Taylor,* exhibition catalogue (Winston-Salem, NC: The Southeastern Center for Contemporary Art, 2011).

44

*Chainlink,* 2008

Wood, veneer, shellac

34 x 46 x 1 in.

Purchased with funds provided by the Windgate Charitable Foundation

# KATIE HUDNALL

b. 1979

American

MFA, Virginia Commonwealth University, Richmond, 2005
BFA, Corcoran College of Art and Design, Washington, DC, 2001

Katie Hudnall regards her work as a metaphor for human relationships. The imperfect edge of one piece fits perfectly against the imperfect edge of another; they are on the verge of collapse, but never quite succumb. She assembles the sculptures using traditional joinery techniques, recycled wood and hardware to convey a sense of use and history. She is head of the wood program at Murray State University in Kentucky.

Collection: Arkansas Art Center, Little Rock.

45
*Bolt Reliquary*, 2011
Recycled wood, mixed media
62 x 40 x 15 in.
Purchased with funds provided by the Windgate Charitable Foundation

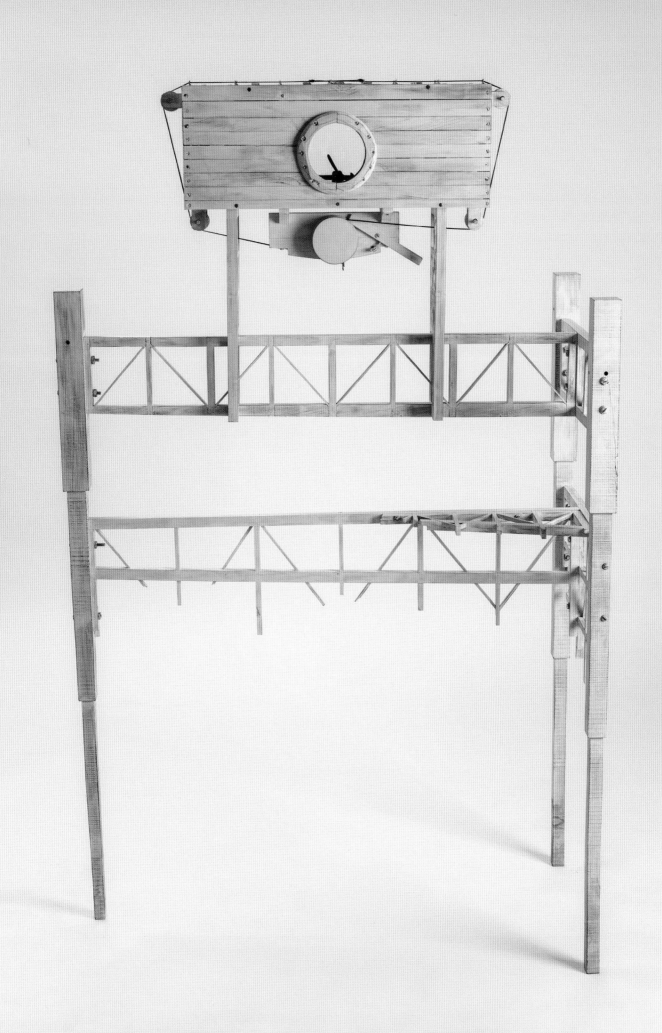

# MARC RICOURT

b. 1963

French

Marc Ricourt lives and works near Dijon, France, and sources the material for his organic wooden objects from his surroundings. He turns local woods on the lathe and then intricately carves and treats the surfaces through bleaching, dying, or the application of ferrous oxide. Ricourt seeks to find a perfect harmony between wood, shape, texture, and color. The history of the utilitarian object and vessel is the starting point for his work.

Collections: Musée du Pays de L'Ain, Bourg-en-Bresse, France; Wood Turning Center, Lewes, Sussex, England.

Reference: Terry Martin and Kevin Wallace, "Marc Ricourt: The Vessel Was Mankind's First Tool," *New Masters of Woodturing: Expanding The Boundaries of Wood Art* (East Petersburg, PA: Fox Chapel Publishing, 2008), 169–174.

**46**

*Lime Wood Sculpture*, 2011

Lime wood, oxide

7¼ x 13½ x 12 in.

Purchased with funds provided by the Windgate Charitable Foundation

# DAVID ROWE

b. 1982

American

MFA, Indiana University, Bloomington, 2009

BFA, University of Illinois, Champaign-Urbana, 2005

David Rowe constructs physical representations of the Midwestern landscape with abandoned industrial structures, using traditional construction techniques and found materials. The landscapes are formed by the artist's perceptions and memories, and become reimagined, reinterpreted vestiges of the past. He was awarded the Efroymson Contemporary Artist Fellowship in 2011. Rowe is a visiting professor at Indiana University in Bloomington.

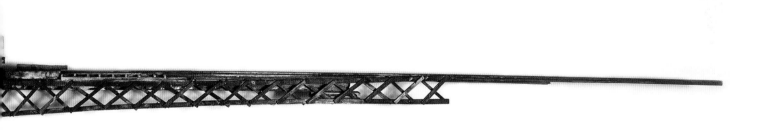

47

Untitled, 2011

Recycled wood, mixed media

40 x 140 x 20 in.

Purchased with funds provided by the
Windgate Charitable Foundation

# MATTHIAS PLIESSNIG

b. 1978

American

MFA, University of Wisconsin-Madison, 2008

BFA, Rhode Island School of Design, Providence, 2003

Computer technology, woodworking, and design intersect in the furniture created by Matthias Pliessnig. Working predominantly with steam-bent wood, Pliessnig constructs sinuous and kinetic forms that draw upon and exceed computer-based design. Working out of his studio in Philadelphia, Pliessnig collaborates with architects on large-scale installations and produces privately commissioned work.

Collections: Museum of Arts and Design, NY; Smithsonian American Art Museum, Washington, DC; James A. Michener Art Museum, Doylestown, PA.

48

*Brace*, 2012

White oak, copper

17 x 88 x 39 in.

Commissioned with funds by the Windgate Charitable Foundation

130

# FIBER

Mark Newport
*Two Gun Kid*, 2006 (detail)
Embroidered comic book cover

# ED ROSSBACH

1914–2002

American

MFA, Cranbrook Academy of Art, Bloomfield Hills, MI, 1947
MFA, Columbia University, Chicago, IL, 1941
BFA, University of Washington, Seattle, 1940

Ed Rossbach was a seminal fiber artist who studied and employed both basket-making and weaving techniques. Originally from Chicago, he was stationed in the Aleutian Islands during WWII and then studied at Cranbrook Academy of Art on the GI Bill. He was drawn to non-traditional materials, including foil, plastic bags, Mylar, twigs, staples, Styrofoam, and twine. He taught at the University of California, Berkeley for twenty-nine years and authored several books on basketry, most notably *The Nature of Basketry* and *Baskets as Textile Art*.

Collections: Metropolitan Museum of Art, NY: Museum of Arts and Design, NY; Oakland Museum of California; the Museum of Modern Art, NY.

References: Ed Rossbach, interview by Carole Austin, Aug. 27–29, 2002, unpublished transcript, Archives of American Art, Smithsonian Institution.

*Ties That Bind: Fiber Art by Ed Rossbach and Katherine Westphal From The Daphne Fargo Collection* (Providence, RI: Museum of Art, Rhode Island School of Design, 1997).

49

*Pete Rose*, 1982
Folded newspaper strips, paint
6¾ x 6¾ x 6⅞ in.
Purchased with funds provided by the ASU Art Museum Store

134

50
*Japanese Plaited Basket*, 1987
Stapled rag paper
11½ x 12 x 12 in.
Gift of Janet and Roger Robinson

# JOANNE SEGAL BRANDFORD

1933–1994

American

MA, University of California, Berkeley, 1967
BA, University of California, Berkeley, 1955

Joanne Segal Brandford was an artist, scholar, teacher, and curator. Her work was driven by her interest and proficiency in global textiles, especially those of North, Central, and Andean America. Her inventive nets and sculptural forms were made by "interlacing, knotting, and twining of primarily natural materials, sometimes dyed." She taught at many colleges across the country including the University of California at Berkeley; Rhode Island School of Design; Montclair State College in New Jersey; and Massachusetts College of Art.

Brandford's awards include a New York State Artists Grant, Basket Maker-in-Residence at Manchester Polytechnic in England, Fellow at the Bunting Institute at Radcliffe College, and Research Fellow in Textile Art at the Peabody Museum of Archaeology and Ethnology at Harvard. Brandford's legacy includes the Brandford/ Elliott Award for Excellence in Fiber Art, which is presented annually by the Textile Society of America.

Collections: Smithsonian American Art Museum, Washington, DC; Racine Art Museum, WI.

Reference: Barbara Goldberg, "Joanne Segal Brandford," *Textile Society of America Symposium Proceedings,* 2004. Paper 450, 202–209. http://digitalcommons.unl.edu/tsaconf/450. (accessed January 2, 2013.)

51
*Basket-figure*, 1983
Fiber
15½ x 13³/₈ x 4¾ in.
Diane and Sandy Besser Collection

# LILLIAN ELLIOTT

1930–1994

American

MFA, Cranbrook Academy of Art, Bloomfield Hills, MI, 1955
BA, Wayne State University, Detroit, MI, 1952

Beginning in 1983 and ending with Lillian Elliott's death in 1994, she and Pat Hickman collaborated in making art. Elliott built reed basketry structures that Hickman covered with hog gut, which, when dry, became a taut skin that pulled the structures tight. The two artists began working almost by accident when Elliott talked of covering a frame with paper and Hickman suggested gut instead. Pat Hickman commented on her collaborator's style, "Her work consistently had a connecting thread back through textile history and forward into new territory."[1]

Basketmaking offered Elliott a dramatic shift from her mainstay technique of weaving. Baskets also allowed her to work large and in the round, simultaneously on an entire surface. From 1955 to 1958, she worked as a designer for the styling division of the Ford Motor Company in Dearborn, Michigan. Elliott taught part-time at numerous institutions in California and influenced several generations of artists in the Bay Area and beyond.

Collections: Smithsonian American Art Museum, Washington, DC; Museum of Arts and Design, NY; Museum of Fine Arts, Boston.

Reference: Pat Hickman, "Lillian Elliott," *Textile Society of America Symposium Proceedings.* 2004, Paper 451. (http://digital commonsunl.edu/tsaconf/451)

# PAT HICKMAN

b. 1941

American

MA, University of California, Berkeley, 1977
BA, University of Colorado, Boulder, 1962

Pat Hickman was first introduced to traditional weaving techniques while she was teaching English at a Turkish girl's school in Istanbul. She returned to the United States and studied textiles with Joanne Segal Brandford and Lillian Elliott. Hickman formed lasting friendships with both artists, sharing studio space with Joanne and eventually collaborating with Elliott. Hickman has worked with numerous organic materials, including gut and skin, to construct her vessel forms in two- and three-dimensions. Hickman relocated to Honolulu in the 1990s when she was offered a full-time teaching position in the Art Department of the University of Hawaii, where she ran the fiber program for sixteen years.

Collections: Philadelphia Museum of Art; Racine Art Museum, WI; Savaria Museum, Szombathely, Hungary.

Reference: "Artist Profile: Pat Hickman," National Basketry Organization, http://nationalbasketry.org/artist-profile-pat-hickman. Accessed November 5, 2012,

Lillian Elliott (l), Pat Hickman (r)

52
*Shaped Bark*, 1991
Bark, linen
10 x 22 x 20 in.
Gift of Sara and David Lieberman

53
*Walk in the Woods*, 1986
Hog gut, sticks
16 x 9 x 9 in.
Gift of Janet and Roger Robinson

# DOROTHY GILL BARNES

b. 1927

American

MA, University of Iowa, Iowa City, 1951
BA, University of Iowa, Iowa City, 1949

Dorothy Gill Barnes credits John Shulze from the University of Iowa as one of her first influential teachers. She took her first weaving class from Ruth Mary Papenthein from Ohio State University, and began incorporating natural materials shortly after mastering the warp and the weft of the loom.

Growing her own materials is an integral part of Barnes's artistic process. In order to imbue her work with a sense of place, Barnes gathers her materials from her local environment, and in order to limit her impact, only gathers materials during the spring and summer months. She continues to employ new processes and materials while sustaining the level of innovation that has been evident in her work from her earlier explorations.

Considered one of the most influential makers within the basket field in recent years, Barnes was presented with the lifetime achievement award in 1993 by the National Museum of Women in the Arts, Washington, DC.

Collections: Museum of Arts and Design, NY; Arkansas Arts Center, Little Rock; Racine Art Museum, WI.

Reference: Dorothy Gill Barnes, Interview by Joanne Cubbs, May 2–7, 2003, unpublished transcript, Archives of American Art, Smithsonian Institution.

54

*Coiled Banyan*, 1988

Banyan

7 x 25 x 25 in.

Diane and Sandy Besser Collection

# JOHN GARRETT

b. 1950

American

MA, University of California, Los Angeles, 1976
BA, Claremont McKenna College, Claremont, CA, 1972

John Garrett was raised in southern New Mexico by parents who were both educators. He developed an appreciation for the hand-made through his parents' collection of Native American arts and crafts. Over the past twenty-five years, Garrett has worked in two- and three-dimensional formats to create textile forms using a variety of materials, such as nails, washers, corks, painted aluminum, copper, and bed springs. These unusual materials may be woven, wrapped, riveted, painted, nailed, stitched, or tied.

Collections: Albuquerque Museum, NM; Detroit Institute of Arts; High Museum, Atlanta.

Reference: *Meeting Ground: Basketry Traditions and Sculptural Forms,* exhibition catalogue (Tempe, AZ and St. Louis, MO: Arizona State University and The Forum, 1990), 8, 14.

55
*Triumph*, 1991
Copper, glass beads
14½ x 19 x 19 in.
Diane and Sandy Besser Collection

# JOHN MCQUEEN

b. 1943

American

MFA, Tyler School of Art, Temple University, Philadelphia, 1975
BA, University of South Florida, Tampa, 1971

John McQueen uses branches, bark, and other natural materials to create basket-like forms that reside in the space between craft, sculpture, and conceptual art. He began his career by studying textiles with Adela Akers at the Tyler School of Art and was further inspired by the Native American baskets that he viewed while living in New Mexico. Many of his works contain text or the human figure, and are containers of existential and poetic ideas.

Collections: Cooper Hewitt Museum, Smithsonian Institution, NY; Philadelphia Museum of Art; Kustindustrimuseum, Trondheim, Norway.

References: Kelly Leigh Mitchell, "John McQueen," *Philadelphia Museum of Art Bulletin* 87, no. 371/372 (Autumn 1991): 34.

Gerald Mead, "Weaving Between the Lines," *Artvoice Weekly* 5, no 23 (June 8, 2006): 18.

56
*CULTIVAR* "a tree can't but be," 1992
Plywood, screws
60 x 24 x 27 in.
Gift of Sara and David Lieberman

# KAY SEKIMACHI

b. 1926

American

MFA, California College of the Arts, Oakland, 1955
BFA, California College of the Arts, Oakland, 1949

Kay Sekimachi pursued most of her artistic education in San Francisco, where she was born and raised. She considers Jack Lenor Larsen, whom she met in the summer of 1956 while teaching at Haystack Mountain School of Crafts, Maine, to be a significant mentor and artistic influence. Sekimachi mastered a variety of techniques and materials to create her vessels, double-weave books and woven boxes.

Sekimachi has been the recipient of several prestigious awards, including the Gold Medal from the American Craft Council, 2002; the Honor Award from the Women's Caucus for Art, 1997; and an Artist Fellowship from the National Endowment for the Arts in 1985.

Collections: Contemporary Art Museum, Honolulu; Musée des arts décoratifs, Paris; Metropolitan Museum of Art, NY.

References: Judith Penny Burton, "Progressional Journeys: Compelling New Directions for Three 'New Basketry' Artists," *Textile Society of America Symposium Proceedings* (2010) Paper 11. http://digitalcommons.unl.edu/tsaconf/11 (accessed June 28, 2012).

Kay Sekimachi (Stocksdale), interview by Suzanne Baizerman, July 26 and Aug. 6, 2001, unpublished transcript, Archives of American Art, Smithsonian Institution.

57

*Washi Vessel*, circa 1995
Antique Japanese paper, folded and machine stitched
22 x 6 x 6 in.
Gift of Sara and David Lieberman

# JERRY BLEEM

b. 1954

American

MFA, The School of the Art Institute of Chicago, 1992
M. Div., Catholic Theological Union at Chicago, 1982
BA, Quincy University, Quincy, IL, 1976

Jerry Bleem is an artist, teacher, writer, Franciscan friar and Catholic priest. In addition to his MFA, Bleem also received his Master's of Divinity, from the Catholic Theological Union of Chicago. As an artist, Bleem examines the cultural construction of meaning by looking at what we discard and how over time, we transform the non-precious through intensive accumulation. His work highlights the relationship between value and identity, and questions assumed ideals. The resulting work, incorporating both two- and three-dimensional surfaces, mines topics ranging from apprehension to beauty, ecology, art, and politics.

He has been awarded numerous fellowships and residencies from the Illinois Arts Council, Arts Midwest, and NEA Regional Visual Arts Council, and the Roswell Artist-in-Residence Grant. Bleem is Professor for the Department of Fiber and Material Studies at the School of the Art Institute of Chicago.

Collections: Anderson Museum of Contemporary Art, Roswell, NM; Arkansas Arts Center, Little Rock.

Reference: http://media.uoregon.edu/channel/2013/02/25/jerry-bleem-visiting-artists-lecture/

58
*Weight/Wait*, 1998
Business cards, wax, acrylic medium,
staples, stone
6 ¼ x 12 ¼ x 5 in.
Gift of the artist

# FERNE JACOBS

b. 1942

American

MFA, Claremont Graduate University, Claremont, CA, 1976

Ferne Jacobs was born in Chicago to parents who had emigrated
from Eastern Europe. She began her career as a painter, exploring the
possibilities of three-dimensional painting before transitioning to weaving. Jacobs constructs three-dimensional sculptures using a simple
weaving technique of wrapping waxed-linen thread around a cord.
Working with fiber and ancient basket-making techniques, Jacobs feels
deeply connected to the earth and its rhythms.

Collections: Smithsonian American Art Museum, Washington, DC: Metropolitan
Museum of Art, NY; Mint Museum of Craft and Design, NC.

Reference: Ferne Jacobs, interview by Mija Ridel, Aug. 30–31, 2005, unpublished
transcript, Archives of American Art, Smithsonian Institution.

59
*Tides,* 2003
Waxed linen thread
26 x 17 x 17 in.
Promised gift of Sara and David Lieberman

# GYÖNGY LAKY

b. 1944

Hungarian, resides in the United States

MA, University of California, Berkeley, 1971

BA, University of California, Berkeley, 1970

Gyöngy Laky is an environmentalist, educator, and San Francisco–based sculptor. Her works are primarily assembled from organic debris and tree prunings that she collects from the many tons of cuttings discarded from local parks, streets, and gardens. Laky's freestanding and wall hanging works are inspired by language and architecture. She strives to change the way we perceive and interact with our natural environment, leveraging craft and language to drive home a point. Laky founded the internationally recognized Fiberworks, Center for the Textile Arts, in Berkeley where she established accredited undergraduate and graduate programs in the mid-1970s. Laky is professor emeritus of the University of California, Davis, where she taught 1978–2005, helping to launch the Department of Environmental Design and serving as the chair in the Department of Art.

Collections: San Francisco Museum of Modern Art; Smithsonian American Art Museum, Washington, DC. Philadelphia Museum of Art.

Reference: Mija Riedel, "Constructing the Unexpected," *American Craft* 69, no. 2 (Apr/May 2009): 54–61.

**60**
*Linkage*, 2005
Manzanita, red ink, metal screws
47 x 47 x 4½ in.
Promised gift of Sara and David Lieberman

# LISA TELFORD

b. 1957

American, Haida

Lisa Telford was born into a remarkable family of Haida basket weavers in Ketchikan, Alaska that includes her grandmother, mother, aunt, cousins, and daughter. Telford celebrates the beauty inherent in nature by harvesting and preparing her materials, including red and yellow cedar bark and spruce root. Her practice incorporates both contemporary and historical weaving techniques associated with her Haida lineage.

She is the recipient of several prestigious awards including Artist-in-residence at the National Museum of the American Indian and the Southwestern Association for Indian Arts Fellowship.

Collections: Hallie Ford Museum of Art, Willamette University, Salem, OR; National Museum of the American Indian, Smithsonian Institution, Washington, DC; Heard Museum, Phoenix, AZ.

61
*Moon Warrior*, 2005
Red cedar bark, cordage, abalone buttons
25 x 14 x 9 in.
Promised gift of Sara and David Lieberman

# LEON NIEHUES

b. 1951

American

Leon Niehues makes baskets from young white oaks that grow in the Ozarks, near where he lives in northwest Arkansas. While using traditional splint techniques, he has added innovative ideas and designs that dramatically change his baskets into exciting contemporary pieces.

In 2005 he was named an Arkansas Living Treasure by the Department of Heritage. In 2012 he was awarded a United States Artist Fellowship.

Collection: Smithsonian American Art Museum, Washington, DC

Reference: Werner Trieschmann, "Leon Niehues: Weave Master," *American Craft* 58, no. 5 (Oct/Nov 1998): 58-61.

62

*Warrior*, 2009

Oak strips, emery cloth, metal rivets

16 x 13 x 13 in.

Gift of Robyn and John Horn

# JARBAS LOPES

b. 1964

Brazilian

BFA, Escola de Belas Artes, Universidade Federal do
Rio de Janeiro, Brazil

Jarbas Lopes is known for collaborative projects that combine both idealistic and practical ambitions and include sculpture, performance, and social practice. Lopes is largely concerned with issues of sustainability in the face of rapid urban growth, due to his first-hand experiences growing up in Rio de Janeiro, one of the largest cities in the world. His ongoing project, *Cicloviaéra*, promotes the bicycle as an alternative form of transportation in congested urban areas. Lopes weaves osier, a flexible natural fiber, around the bicycle in a way that still allows it to function.

Collections: Museum of Modern Art, NY; Victoria and Albert Museum, London; Associacão Brasileira de Artes em São Paulo, Brazil.

Reference: *Jarbas Lopes: Cicloviaéra*, exhibition catalogue (Tempe: AZ: Arizona State University Art Museum, 2008).

63

*Cicloviaéra*, 2006

Osier (natural fiber vine) over bicycle

42 x 72 x 20½ in.

Purchased with funds provided by the Herbert H. and Barbara C. Dow Foundation

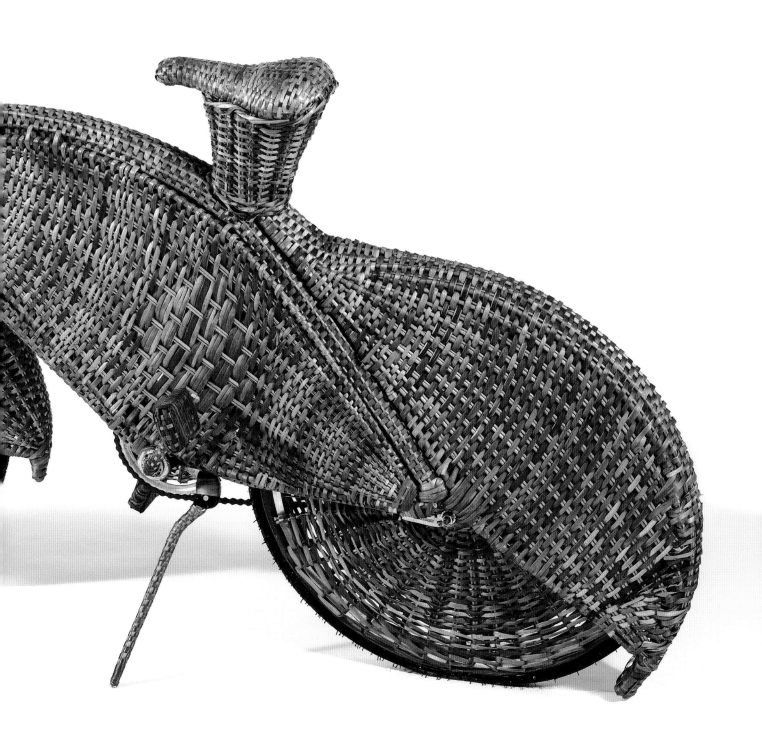

# MARK NEWPORT

b. 1964

American

MFA, School of the Art Institute of Chicago, Chicago, 1991
BFA, Kansas City Art Institute, Kansas City, 1986

Mark Newport knits acrylic superhero costumes that question the roles of gender and masculinity in contemporary culture. The costumes, created in human scale as wearable objects, challenge the standard muscular form of the hero and ask the viewer to imagine him or herself wearing the costume and transforming into hero. Newport is the Artist-in-residence and Head of Fiber at the Cranbrook Academy of Art.

Collections: Whitney Museum of American Art, NY; Detroit Institute of Arts; Racine Art Museum, WI.

References: Kim Humphries, "Mark Newport Explores Modern-day Heroes in Laumeier Exhibition," Artdaily.org, http://www.artdaily.org/index.asp?int sec=2&int new=35837 (accessed January 25, 2010)

Sarah Tanguy, "Staged Stories," American Craft 69, no. 6 (December/January 2010): 38–39.

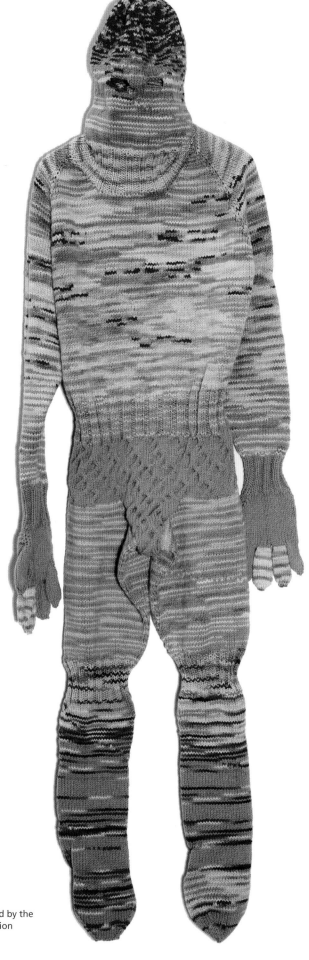

64

*W Man,* 2009

Hand-knit acrylic, buttons

80 x 23 x 6 in.

Purchased with funds provided by the Windgate Charitable Foundation

65

*Two Gun Kid*, 2006

Embroidered comic book cover

11 x 7 in.

Purchased with funds provided by the
Windgate Charitable Foundation

# SONYA CLARK

b. 1967

American

MFA, Cranbrook Academy of Art, Bloomfield Hills, MI 1995
BFA, School of the Art Institute of Chicago, 1993
BA, Amherst College, Amherst, MA, 1989

Sonya Clark creates textile works, sculptures, installations, and photographs. She uses hair and plastic combs as materials to address issues of race and identity in her work. Guided by her craft tendencies, Clark configures fine-toothed combs in cloth and uses hair as a medium for fiber art and readymade portraits.

Born in Washington, DC, Clark is the Chair of the Department of Craft/ Material Studies at Virginia Commonwealth University in Richmond. She has been awarded several honors including the Pollock-Krasner Award, Red Gate Residency in China, Smithsonian Artist Research Fellowship, and most recently named a United States Artist Fellow grant recipient.

Collections: Cranbrook Art Museum, Bloomfield Hills, MI; Indianapolis Museum of Art; Madison Museum of Contemporary Art, WI.

References: Christy DeSmith, "Data Processing: The New Materiality, Digital Dialogues at the Boundaries of Contemporary Craft," *American Craft* (December/ January 2011): 24–25.
B.A. Harrington, "'New Materiality' and the Sensory Power of Craft," *Furniture Matters* (September 2010): 6–7.

66
*Threadwrapped in Blue and Brown*, 2008
Combs, thread
60 x 45 x 1 in.
Purchased with funds provided by the Windgate Charitable Foundation

# MARGARITA CABRERA

b. 1973

Mexican, resides in the United States.

MFA, Hunter College of the City University of New York, NY, 2001
BFA, Hunter College of the City University of New York, NY, 1997

Margarita Cabrera's work addresses sociopolitical issues within local communities, including aspects of immigration, violence, and the economic relationship between the United States and Mexico. Cabrera creates textile and ceramic- based sculptures that replicate specific cultural objects, which hold significant meaning for the Mexican community. She was born in Monterrey Nuevo Leon, Mexico, and lived in Mexico City for ten years, then immigrated to the US with her family. In 2012, she was a recipient of the Knight Artist in Residence at the Mc-Coll Center for Visual Art in Charlotte, NC.

Collections: El Museo del Barrio, NY; Museum of Fine Art, Houston, TX; University of California, Riverside.

References: Gabriel Craig, "Manufacturing Interventions," *Fiber Arts* 37, no. 3 (November/December, 2010): 36-37.
Sasha Bergrstrom-Katz, "Interview with Margarita Cabrera," *ArtSlant*, accessed December 20, 2012, http://www.artslant.com/la/articles/show/1654/.

**67**

*Space in Between- Nopal #3*, 2012

Fabric (border patrol uniform), thread, copper, terracotta pot

41 x 59 x 34 in.

Purchased with funds provided by the Windgate Charitable Foundation

# CAROL ECKERT

b. 1945

American

BA, Arizona State University, Tempe, 1967

Carol Eckert began working with fiber while teaching art classes in the late 1960s at the City of Phoenix community arts center. She first explored fiber materials using traditional basketry technique in which stitches are knotted around a fiber core. Later, she invented a technique using wire as the core, allowing her to create three-dimensional figures. Her compositions have primarily focused on animal imagery found in world myths and cultures. Eckert has taught workshops at Arrowmont School of Arts and Crafts and Haystack Mountain School of Crafts and participated in exhibitions across the United States and abroad.

Collections: Denver Art Museum, CO; Mint Museum of Craft and Design, Charlotte, NC; Smithsonian American Art Museum. Washington, DC.

Reference: Carol Eckert, interview by Jo Lauria, June 18–19, 2007, unpublished transcript, Archives of American Art, Smithsonian Institution.

68

*And a Wolf Shall Devour the Sun*, 2012
Black waxed linen thread, wire
14 x 65 x 3 in.
Anonymous Gift

# MATERIAL EVOLUTION

## THE FUTURE OF CONTEMPORARY CRAFT

by Elizabeth Kozlowski

TO INVESTIGATE THE IDEA OF "RETHINKING CRAFT," the curatorial staff of the ASU Art Museum looked at the current structure of media-based programs at other national universities. The move to increase theory-based study outside of the traditional studio artist model is significant. In this shifting paradigm universities are producing exemplary MFA graduates at an increasing rate. The following programs stand out in the pedagogy of craft disciplines: Cranbrook Academy of Art in Bloomfield, MI; Virginia Commonwealth University in Richmond; University of the Arts in Philadelphia; and the University of Wisconsin at Madison. These educational institutions, and programs within and outside of the larger schools of art, have created a network of individuals who are making substantial work and sharing their passion and influence with the current generation of students.

In an effort to expand the permanent collection of contemporary craft at the ASU Art Museum, we asked professors at these universities to recommend current and recent graduate students who are creating compelling work. We soon realized that the educators at the epicenter of these university systems could not be ignored due to the strength of their own work. These artists and their students suggest the future of craft in physical form.

Craft as a tool for action is central to most professional practices in universities. Both technical skill and the concept to back it up are required to create a physical representation of the artist's ideal or not-so-ideal world. Whether deconstructing the object—as Anders Ruhwald, head of the ceramics department at Cranbrook Academy, does in his work—or layering an everyday object with gender and racial meaning—as Sonya Clark, head of the fiber department at VCU, does—craft is no longer viewed outside of the context of art. The level of innovation and experimentation in craft-based studies has produced a hybrid of material and concept that engenders its own model in contemporary art.

In keeping with the spirit of rethinking and the continued reexamination of crafts as a significant and essential part of the arts, we asked a broad spectrum of leaders in the field to present their individual viewpoints on the state of contemporary craft. The following perspectives on where this hybridized world of making is headed range from emphasis on the influence of educational systems to new technologies that are driving fabrication. While these philosophies are varied in scope, it is readily apparent that traditional frameworks are breaking down. In this evolutionary period, as art, craft, design, and concept are reevaluated, the artists in this exhibition, and in the field at large, illustrate the complex nature and expanding boundaries of contemporary art.

## MUSHINESS

by Anders Ruhwald

In writing on the future of craft I must acknowledge that my field of vision is limited by my own experience. My practice is primarily engaged with issues that broadly concern the nature of everyday objects and ceramics. As such, it is situated somewhere in the grey area between art, craft, and design. While my work may at times brush up against the broader scope of craft, what I do cannot be understood solely through this lens. I have constructed this limitation consciously: I find the idea of craft to be conceptually enriching yet the crafts as such seem too narrow to cover what I think should be considered ceramics. My point is that while ceramics may be one of the main constituents of crafts, the field of crafts does not serve as an umbrella for ceramics as such. The discourse on the relationship between material and artist can help us understand some aspects of ceramics, but the discussions within the craft field often feel too narrow and a poor fit for the whole subject of ceramics.

As an artist, it is hard for me to imagine the field of ceramics without the connection to the discourse of crafts. But as Paul Greenhalgh points out, "Ceramics is a plural activity."[1] As such it is impossible to understand the practices of ceramics through the narrow institutional definitions of craft, art, or design. The history of ceramics is messy; it is perceived as lowbrow, technique-ridden, domestic, decorative and object-driven. But that discourse between craft and ceramics is why the material is currently enjoying much attention from the world of art and design. Now ceramics curiously finds most cultural resonance when it is appropriated into the world of design and art that is not so defined. Look at the work of Nicole Cherubini, Maarten Baas or Grayson Perry and you get my point.

If the craft field is to have a future, it must be understood as part of a whole rather than in isolation. In the struggle to define itself craft ends up excluding important tributaries to the main narrative. For example, Jeff Koons' work doesn't seem to fit within the late twentieth-century understanding of crafts, although it really should. Hereby the discourse of craft becomes narrow and too limiting for artists like me to be comfortably framed by. In my opinion the future lies in expanding the understanding of crafts. This can only come from within the field itself, by allowing the practices that exist in the boundaries of the field to take center stage. Crafts really need mushy boundaries.

1. Paul Greenhalgh, "Discourse and Decoration," in Garth Clark, ed., *Ceramic Millennium: Critical Writings on Ceramic History, Theory, and Art* (Halifax, NS: Press of the Nova Scotia College of Art and Design, 2006), 168.

**Anders Ruhwald** graduated from the Royal College of Art, London in 2005. His work is represented in private and public collections internationally including the Victoria and Albert Museum (UK), Icheon World Ceramic Center (Rep. of South Korea), the Detroit Institute of Arts, and the National Museum of Sweden. Currently he is the Artist-in-Residence and Head of the Ceramics Department at Cranbrook Academy of Art in Michigan.

## IN THE HANDS OF THE CURIOUS

by Sonya Clark

Curiosity. Without it, all creativity gets stuck. The future of craft is in the hands of the curious. Embracing it as a core value is the best thing we do. This is confirmed in my daily life as an educator and artist. The students I have had the privilege to teach—at Virginia Commonwealth University, the University of Wisconsin, Madison, and elsewhere—constantly infect me with their curiosity. I am gratefully refreshed and renewed. The most memorable critiques in my own education—at the School of the Art Institute of Chicago and Cranbrook Academy of Art—were marked by the curiosity of my peers and mentors. I have come to measure the success of an artist's talk by the quality and/or quantity of the questions poised. I'm enamored with the surprising questions that I do not readily have answers for, the ones that gnaw at me. These propel the work forward and ignite my own curiosity.

When craft is in dialogue with its audience, it does not and cannot stagnate. The fresh flowing water of our field turns fetid when we as makers and audience assume, shut down, impose strict limitations, or end every thought or art work with a period rather than a question mark. The common denominator among experts, innovators, and outliers is curiosity. Experts with years of embodied knowledge intertwine curiosity with persistence. Sometimes, there are small shifts in the studio; other times, seismic shifts. A level of inquiry is a constant force. Innovators dissect a precept and build from their discoveries, while outliers use curiosity to build bridges between their primary interests and others. The majority of artists I know combine aspects of these qualities.

As artists, we establish rules and impose limitations that define the territory of our art practice. We freely play once those rules are clearly defined. If the game gets boring, we can alter any of the rules and get ourselves unstuck. We are shortsighted and narrow-minded if we locate the beginnings of craft history in the European Arts and Craft movement of the late 1800s. Our history is vast, global, and diverse; encyclopedic collecting institutions like the Metropolitan Museum of Art might as well be called the Metropolitan Museum of Craft given their holdings. Where do we find craft? I believe everywhere. It is not hemmed in by history, material, theory, or technique, rather, it is deeply integrated. Like a tree, the depth and breadth of craft's roots extend across cultures and time, into the far reaches of material culture and art history. Those deep and extensive origins provide stability for more extensive branches. We can extend ourselves nimbly because we have so much history to draw upon. Artists can question, challenge, integrate, and sustain what craft will become because we have such an enduring past. Curiosity is our sap.

In 2006 **Sonya Clark** joined the faculty at Virginia Commonwealth University as chair the Department of Craft/Material Studies. Previously, Clark was Baldwin-Bascom Professor of Creative Arts at the University of Wisconsin-Madison where she taught for ten years in Design Studies. Before that, Clark earned her MFA from the Cranbrook Academy of Art, BFA from the Art Institute of Chicago, and BA from Amherst College. Clark was the recipient of the 2011 United States Artist Fellowship.

## POP! GOES CRAFT

by Sandra Alfoldy

What does the dog do when it finally catches the car? After decades of occupying a marginalized position, the crafts have exploded onto the arts scene and into popular consciousness. It is everywhere—from major art exhibitions to McDonald's. The ubiquitous fast-food chain is rolling out a major campaign that includes giving away free, reusable ceramic coffee mugs by the French designer Patrick Norguet. For one important reason the craft field must move quickly to capitalize on this resurgence of interest from such diverse constituencies: control. Otherwise the dog will be dragged for miles behind the car.

The final decades of the twentieth century were spent defining studio craft. This became an official movement for national organizations like the American Craft Council. Studio makers became the gods and goddesses of the craft world. Benchmarks for specific materials were cemented into place through the development of specialized groups like National Council on Education for the Ceramic Arts, Society of North American Goldsmiths, and the Textile Society of America and writings on craft reflected the supremacy of the studio movement.

Around five years ago things started to change. A new perspective on craft emerged: craft is everything. The boundaries established by studio craft were erased in favor of an openness that suggested craft is part of the larger visual arts world. At the same time, thinkers like Richard Sennett advocated for craftsmanship as "an enduring, basic human impulse," that can be applied onto any aspect of human endeavor from software development to parenting.[1]

Today's general public views craft from new perspectives. In art galleries where sculpture quotes craft materials (without being discussed as craft), at markets as expressions of the power of do-it-yourself in the time of the Great Recession, and in the media as slick marketing. Who doesn't want to buy "Artisan" nacho chips? This is where the car is dragging

the dog down the road. Dedication to the perfection of a single material or the kinaesthetic comforts of human-scale craft objects are thrown aside in favor of sculptural borrowings. Tori Spelling is yelling, "Put down your glue guns," at craftspeople competing on national television as flocks of do-it-yourselfers watch with rapt attention. Most dangerous of all, corporations and advertising agencies have circled around the idea of craft. Rather than being taken up as a battle cry for outstanding skill, quality, and concept (the hallmarks of studio craft), craft has been incorrectly associated with product branding of major companies. It is safe to assume that Bernard Leach would not have enjoyed a Starbuck's Artisanal Breakfast Sandwich.

The future of craft will be determined by whoever controls the message of craft. At this moment when craft has become a popular advertising term, it is imperative that professional craftspeople define their own work and that this is respected by the general public, collectors, curators, and critics. For craft to avoid becoming merely a meaningless advertising pitch, the dog needs to hop into the driver's seat and enjoy the ride.

1. Richard Sennett, *The Craftsman* (New Haven and London: Yale University Press, 2008), 9.

**Dr. Sandra Alfoldy** is Professor of Craft History at NSCAD University and Associate Curator of Fine Craft at the Art Gallery of Nova Scotia. She is the author of *The Allied Arts: Architecture and Craft* (2012), and curator of the Canadian Craft exhibition at the 2010 Vancouver Winter Olympics, and the 2009 Cheongju International Craft Biennale. Alfoldy received her Ph.D. from Concordia University in 2001.

## A CREATIVE CONCEPT

by Rose B. Simpson

To craft is to create. To create is to manifest a new object, a new objective, a new perspective, a new reality and a new future. A discerning eye is a visionary crafter, one who observes thoroughly and creates consciously. Whether it is internal or external, the creator is a journeyman/woman searching for the road most illuminating. As crowded as the contemporary creative world is, it can be a lonely voyage and by far the most personal.

One of the primary issues I have with social education is that it informs what has already been done, thereby creating a stifling environment in which the artist assumes he or she must push beyond their innate desire for fear of not making something noteworthy. One of the greatest things about education is that it honors prior innovations, thereby inspiring and challenging the student to build upon this abundant history, empowering the student to write the next chapter in the book of creativity.

When I witness an incredible spark of creativity from another person, I find myself wishing I had thought of that idea. Previous examples that have been released into the eternal human consciousness, irrespective of their origins, assist us on the path of discovering an overabundance of perspectives housed in books, museums, online, or local art or craft shows. We are gifted access to a dynamic landscape that becomes more cluttered with objects as our creative types grow and evolve. How do we honor this history and bear the responsibility to carry it forward into the future with the same intention?

Making a decision to challenge contemporary or historical socio-cultural patterns requires us to question our own dependable modes of thinking. In doing so, we will inevitably find ourselves on the road less traveled. This path may be most unnerving, testing our humanity, but it also has the potential to be most rewarding.

As I continue to craft my life in new and challenging directions, I find the most unique story is one that is true to me. Not only is it incredibly personal, but it holds the potential to transcend to universal themes. The more I bravely travel into my inner self, the more honest and inclusive it can be.

May we all choose a path less traveled. If we choose to question ourselves, our cultures, societies, and belief systems, we can remember how to be passionately creative again. As we challenge our abilities and find faith in our voice, our ideas become more than an object we craft. This process becomes a way of life.

**Rose Simpson** is the daughter of clay sculptor Roxanne Swentzell and mixed-media artist Patrick Simpson. After studying at the University of New Mexico, Albuquerque,and the Institute of American Indian Arts in Santa Fe, she received a BFA in Studio Arts in 2007, and an Honors MFA in Ceramics from the Rhode Island School of Design in 2011. Rose Simpson applies her abilities in ceramic and mixed-media sculpture and a variety of other artistic media to explore the relationship between aesthetic expression and life.

## WOODWORKING TODAY

by Matthias Pliessnig

Artists who use wood as their chosen medium have seen the world evolve rapidly in the past two decades. Countless new states of art materials have surfaced; computer-aided design has exploded; and the word "craft" has taken a beating. The woodworking industry has slowly dragged behind contemporary design theory. Contributing to the problem is our education system. I see two types of students: some are instructed to cling onto the traditional ways of using wood and others are embracing new technology without the foundation to understand the characteristics of materials and the rules inherent in them.

This results in works that, at times, are not structurally stable, fall apart, or simply don't push the material conceptually to a relevant conclusion. If we want to see innovative use of wood, the young makers and designers need to learn the rules before they can break them. Oftentimes hands-on instruction is divorced from technology training. It's time to let go of tradition: don't worry, it will always be there! Now we must move forward, teaching the foundations of wood, followed by computer technology, resulting in the adrenalin-filled experimentation of a synergistic relationship between the computer and the chisel.

Computer technology, craft skills, and design meet in the steam-bent wood furniture created by **Matthias Pliessnig.** His works have been exhibited at Salone Internazionale de Mobile in Milan, Wexler Gallery in Philadelphia, International Art & Design Fair in NY, and the Smithsonian American Art Museum in Washington, DC. His sculptural furniture can also be found in the permanent collections of the Museum of Arts and Design in NY and the Smithsonian American Art Museum.

## CRAFT'S BACK IS UP AGAINST THE WALL —OR NOT

by Love Jönsson

"Craft's back is up against the wall," remarked Professor Mike Press in his introduction to the conference at Gray's School of Art in Aberdeen, Scotland, in 2004. I scribbled it down in my notepad, but not without putting a question mark in the margin. As I now review my lecture notes from the conference almost a decade later, I can't help but emphasize the question mark. Can it really be true that craft is in a recession and desperately needs to defend its position? Have not the crafts in the new millennium proved to be vital, attractive, relevant, and even fun?

By watching a video clip from the Aberdeen conference on the web, I realized that Mike Press was not speaking about the crafts as such when he made that comment in 2004,[1] but referred instead to the status of craft courses in the U.K. higher-education system. But this striking image of craft as being pushed back and questioned builds upon a tradition of self-deprecating general descriptions of the field. Ever since the nature and future of craft became a topic of debate in the nineteenth century, makers and theorists have expressed their fears that craft practice is on the downturn, that it is losing its role in society, and that it runs the risk of becoming extinct. The theory that industrialization—and other aspects of modernity—is killing craft has become so widespread that it is taken as truth. It is difficult to imagine a craft discourse that does not start from the assumption that the crafts need to be supported, taken care of, and protected. But maybe time has come to turn the whole issue upside-down.

Today it is obvious that it is not craft production that is on the decline in the Western world, but its industrial counterpart. Factories are closing one after the other, victims of globalization. Craft practice, on the other hand, is flourishing, fueled by the range of possibilities for worldwide communication and promotion that new technology offers. Rather than being a threat to craft, the digital revolution has provided the field with renewed energy and an expanded audience. Simultaneously, movements such as DIY and craftivism have integrated themselves into the larger culture of craft, bringing with them practical methods as well as theoretical perspectives that have revitalized the field as a whole.

Still, the image of craft as pushed up against the wall is notoriously persistent. It is likely that this has to do with the strong notion of the crafts as essentially static. Anything static is bound to disappear if everything around it changes dramatically. The great mistake of the craft debate, repeated over one hundred and fifty years, is its inability to recognize that craft is not static but a dynamic field marked by constant reevaluation and change. There is no need to fear that craft will disappear. The only thing we know about the craft of the future is that it will be, in some parts at least, different from the one of today. It is precisely this flexibility that grants craft its survivability.

1. A video of Mike Press' introduction to the Aberdeen conference (September 8, 2004) can be viewed at: http://www.challengingcraft.org/

**Love Jönsson** is a curator at the Röhsska Museum for Fashion, Design and Decorative Arts in Gothenburg, Sweden. His articles, essays, and reviews on contemporary crafts have appeared in numerous publications both in Sweden and abroad. From 2005 to 2011, he was a visiting lecturer on the history and theory of crafts at the HDK School of Design and Crafts at the University of Gothenburg.

## CRAFTING A FUTURE

by Garth Johnson

The field of craft has a crisis about its place in the world with every new generation. Why aren't people making things anymore? Why aren't people buying handmade things as much as they used to? Why isn't the art world sitting up and noticing us? What the hell are the kids making in art school?

It's 2013, the economy is reeling and over the past several years I have heard makers complaining that whippersnappers on Etsy are lowering their price points and that kids today don't actually collect or buy things—they're content with digitally re-posting things on the internet to their Facebook or Pinterest pages.

At the same time crafters are busy wringing their hands about their declining fortunes, throngs of people are down the street at the local Whole Foods paying top dollar for heirloom fruits and vegetables with the assurance that the food was ethically grown by a cloister of blind nuns downstate. Stories matter and our field isn't doing a good job telling our story—at least not when compared to the local artisan pickle makers that now dot our urban landscape.

The language of craft is being coopted by advertisers. A popular Jeep ad tells us that:

> "The things that make us Americans are the things we make. This has always been a nation of builders, of craftsmen. Men and women for whom straight stitches and clean welds were matters of personal pride... As a people, we do well when we make good things, and not so well when we don't."

If advertisers can sell Jeeps using the language of craft, then surely we can sell craft using the language of craft. By all accounts, the field of craft is flourishing. The online knitting website ravelry.com boasts 2,430,818 users. In the first seven months of 2012 alone, etsy.com boasted 19 million members and sold $436.9 million dollars worth of handmade merchandise. Clearly, people are buying .

Where does this leave the craftsperson who sells labor-intensive fine work to collectors?

The patrons and collectors of fine craft who made the field what it is today are rapidly aging. Fortunately, there is a new generation of buyers that welcome handmade goods. Right now they might be buying iPod cozies decorated with birds, and artisanal pickles, but they're aging too—having families and building careers that will enable them to purchase handmade objects that reflect evolving taste and income levels.

It is craft's job to make these connections. The field of design has done an excellent job of relating to broader audiences through the witty use of function and materials. Designers, like advertisers, have become adept at using storytelling and the language of craft to connect with buyers. The Maker movement is using technology like 3-D printing to empower thousands of people to start tinkering and making things in their garages.

In order to ensure that craft has a bright future, bridges must be built to a new generation of makers and buyers. Fortunately, building is what we do best.

**Garth Johnson** is a studio artist, writer, and educator who lives in Eureka, California. He is a craft activist who explores craft's influence and relevance in the twenty-first century. His first book, *1000 Ideas for Creative Reuse,* was published in 2009. Johnson was guest editor for the Summer 2012 issue of *Studio Potter* magazine.

## THE ARRIVAL OF A NEW RENEGADE

by Faythe Levine

I was invited to speak at the American Craft Council (ACC) conference Creating a New Craft Culture in 2009 during the height of my book tour for *Handmade Nation: The Rise of D.I.Y. Art, Craft and Design* (Princeton Architectural Press). The audience for the book and film grew rapidly, and I became a de facto spokesperson for the emerging craft community. As the Do It Yourself (DIY) or indie craft movement became a hot topic of debate within the larger craft world, I was thrust into the role of spokesperson, a position in which I wasn't particularly comfortable. Regardless of the controversy, there was too much momentum to stop what was unfolding. I tried to represent both sides of the argument objectively, and to get all to consider whether DIY was adding a positive or negative light to craft?

Personally, I was drawn to the impossibility of defining the DIY community. I had no issues until for a lecture to an audience filled with highly educated and opinionated professionals, I was asked to define it. I had a moment of sheer panic, then the lyrics to an old punk song popped into my head, "This is happening without your permission / the arrival of a new renegade."[1] I embraced these lyrics as my mantra and added them to the first slide to set the tone of my talk. There was an audible reaction in the room when that first slide was projected and I began speaking.

*Handmade Nation* was fueled entirely by my passion to draw attention to a community built around a simple idea that one can be empowered by making. My purpose was not to compartmentalize a potential movement. With the lyrics as my inspiration, I decided I would stay elusive about definitions and focus on the amazing variety of talent and power I had witnessed during my research. I found comfort in this description of our generation written by Renwick Gallery curator Nicholas Bell, "Its makers operate in a changed zeitgeist, feel different societal pressures than their forebears and work with a renewed sense of urgency. They have access to new technologies and aren't afraid to use them."[2] This sense of urgency is both productive for emerging works and potentially damaging to past process and knowledge.

I see our future as a constant search for balance between studio work and engagement with online communities. My security blanket for the future is the knowledge that the DIY culture will continue to exist. Wrapped in a "no rules" ethos I can work guiltless, embracing a multi-media studio practice that so many of us now take advantage of. I had not shared the previous line of the song lyrics that saved my day at the ACC conference—"face it you're old and out of touch"—but in this essay I encourage change as we head into uncharted territories. In order to infiltrate and influence all makers, we must push boundaries and predetermined roles within craft. By keeping an open mind about what the future of craft holds—no matter how painful it might be—we will not fall victim to the divide that has threatened past generations.

1. Lyrics from "Her Jazz" written by Huggy Bear, released by Wiiija Records, 1993.

2. Nicholas R. Bell, " Craft Futures: A Generation at Hand," *40 under 40: Craft Futures*, Nicholas R. Bell, Douglas Coupland, Bernard L. Herman and Michael J. Prokopow (Washington, DC: Smithsonian American Art Museum), 14.

**Faythe Levine** is an independent researcher, multimedia artist, curator, author, and collector based in Milwaukee, Wisconsin. Levine's current focus is *Sign Painters*, a documentary and book about the trade of traditional hand lettering in America. Levine curates Sky High Gallery and produces Art vs. Craft, an annual fair held in Milwaukee. Levine's first book and film, *Handmade Nation: The Rise of D.I.Y. Art, Craft and Design*, received widespread critical attention.

## CRAFT: THE FUTURE IN THE MAKING

by Dr. Catharine Rossi

In the late twentieth century craft's demise was repeatedly portended and the very idea of a future negated. Certainly the odds seemed stacked against craft: amidst globalization and relentless technological advance, the scales and values of craft seemed at odds with those of the modern world. Being invited to reflect on its future is therefore a good sign, both of craft's healthy condition today and that it will have a tomorrow.

The present state of the field suggests that a diverse range of methods and materials will be used to make craft in the future. On the one hand, the analog will continue to have value, be it as a site for free experimentation in terms of form, material, and process, or as a set of traditions that makers seek to uphold and renew. The recent upsurge of craft as a handmade technology comes at a time of heightened concerns about the ethical and environmental implications of global capitalism, in which non-exploitative and sustainable associations of low-tech, local production offer an alternative for future manufacturing. We must meet the expectations of craft's claim to moral high ground.

Yet while this manual mode will continue, we live in a digital age that impacts the design, creation, and consumption of craft objects. As Max Fraser, curator of the 2010 exhibition *Labcraft: Digital Adventures in Contemporary Craft*, points out, many practitioners are embracing the possibilities of digital technologies because of the breadth of scales and forms they can produce.[1] These technologies, when used in conjunction with traditional materials and techniques, herald a future in which long-established skills are supplemented by new skills in hacking and tinkering which accompany social ways of making and sharing objects in both the on and offline worlds.[2] Far from sounding the death knell for craft, digitization supports an increasingly central role for the future.

Craft isn't used to being in the limelight. The craft historian Glenn Adamson has argued that craft is not an autonomous field but one that exists in relation to its more conspicuous cousins of art and design.[3] While craft's status in this relationship is bemoaned as subaltern, its social embeddedness has persistently provided craft's expressive power. Disrupting boundaries and disturbing hierarchies through quiet acts of subversion has a long-established place as the more conceptual and political arm of craft's history, from the Arts and Crafts movement at the turn of the twentieth century to the countercultural collectives of the 1970s and today's craftivist provocateurs.

Ultimately, these reflections suggest while the methods may change, the motivations at play in craft's future will have a lot in common with its past. The craft of tomorrow will be collective and creative; it will be a site of alterity and authenticity, of skilled production, and socially committed subversion—just as it has always been.

1. Max Fraser, Lab Craft: *Digital Adventures in Contemporary Craft* (London: Crafts Council, 2010), np. http://www.craftscouncil.org.uk/files/exhibition/aacbfd268dccd335-lab_craft_essay_max-fraser.pdf (accessed 27 September 2012).

2. For more on hacking and online craft communities, see the essays in Daniel Charney, ed., *The Power of Making: The Importance of Being Skilled* London: V&A Publishing, 2011.

3. Glenn Adamson, *Thinking Through Craft* (Oxford; New York: Berg, 2007), 9–37.

A senior lecturer in design history at Kingston University, **Dr. Catharine Rossi** specializes in the history and theory of craft and design and their relationship in the twentieth and twenty-first centuries, and writes extensively on these areas.

## CRAFT'S RESTLESS BOUNDARIES

by Emily Zilber

Many of today's makers and thinkers resist the idea of a distinct crafts field and reject the model of a defined movement, like studio craft, which is the paradigm that has dominated the display of craft in museums. Because museums are centered on discreet objects and naturally inclined toward tradition, they seem increasingly alienated from the future of craft and craft practice. We were therefore encouraged when ASU Art Museum asked us to enter into a contemporary conversation about how to shape—or expand—a symbiotic and supportive relationship with the museum.

First, it is important to recognize the plurality of craft's present. Materials, techniques, and concepts essential to historical definitions of craft are used today by a wide variety of makers, not only by those who self-identify with the craft community. Sampling from ideas connected with art, craft, and design is viewed as a natural, critical action. Craft continues to survive, and thrive within specific forms,

materials, or functions, but it has also become a context for other art practices. It exists as a tool from a larger kit, a set of assumptions to adhere to or to deconstruct, or a history against which one might position oneself. The future of craft defines a spectrum with the crafted object at one end and discussions about craft taking place around, through, and because of that object at the other end.

For some, reaching outside of craft's traditional boundaries for new meaning has indicated craft's end. Reframing this debate through one of craft's great truisms—learning, doing and saying new things through busy hands—suggests a less cynical interpretation. The use of craft in an open context can be seen as a sign of thinking and learning, even though changes are reflected in materials, tools, reasons to make, and categories of making.

The future for collecting museums interested in craft is filled with new challenges and opportunities. How can work be presented in a way that engages in dialogue about the boundaries of craft, respects and adheres to traditional definitions of craft when necessary, and encourages new ways of thinking for a public armed with expectations about what craft is and does? The solution may be to represent a certain degree of interdisciplinarity and subjectivity in the museum, seeking value in both orthodox and unorthodox narratives of craft. This means tempering the questioning path set by today's makers with some degree of categorization, connoisseurship, and curatorial prescription. The museum should welcome the productive uncertainty that marks contemporary craft into its galleries and storerooms, and replace the rigid canon with a conversational one.

The aim must be to place contemporary craft in context, while avoiding the trap of the new.[1] Today's interdisciplinary focus on process, intent, and content in craft, while seemingly a departure, isn't entirely novel. It has many precedents inherent in objects residing in our collections: from William Morris to the mid-century designer-craftsman. Craft curators need to view both contemporary and historical craft as intersecting with an expanded set of narratives. We must also become more adept at addressing critical conversations taking place across slippery boundaries. With clarity and adeptness, we can do our part to encourage dialogue between craft's past and its future in harmony with this moment of creative restlessness.

1. I refer here to a quote from David Levi Strauss: "Without history, 'the new' becomes a trap: a sequential recapitulation of past approaches with no forward movement. It is a terrible thing to be perpetually stuck in the present." In *Head to Hand: Art and the Manual*, Oxford University Press, pg. 155.

**Emily Zilber** is the Ronald L. and Anita C. Wornick Curator of Contemporary Decorative Arts at the Museum of Fine Arts, Boston. Prior to joining the MFA, Zilber was Assistant Curator at Cranbrook Art Museum at the Cranbrook Academy of Art. Zilber holds a BA in art history from the University of Chicago and an MA from the Bard Graduate Center for Decorative Arts, Design History, and Material Culture, NY.

## CRAFTING A CONTINUUM: RETHINKING THE CONTEMPORARY CRAFT FIELD

by Dennis Stevens

The idea of a *continuum* that can be *crafted* prompts me to question whether it is appropriate to assume that our past can link neatly with our future. I tend to be skeptical of the primacy of craft as a way of knowing and yet, I believe fully in the meaningfulness of the handmade art object. This is not a contradiction because craft coexists within a context of object-making where other ways of knowing often intervene in unexpected ways. But, a problem does exist where the teaching of art history conflicts with pedagogical concerns in the practices of teaching and learning of craft. It is a tension between tradition and progress and it is inherently political.

It is a problem of how we view the past and how that view influences our view of our choices in the present. For this reason, I am not convinced that the presumption of craft as a fixed category that requires preservation will yield stability in the future. In this sense, to highlight the celebratory in craft is to downplay the critical, wherein the critical infers an active questioning of assumptions. We must always question ourselves and our practices. I believe that if we view history as a predetermined, sequential progression we risk failing to recognize our own capacity to be active agents in the present. I prefer instead to highlight our choices today. As new technologies emerge, artists, craftspeople, and designers will integrate these tools with current practices and create new ways of working. Faculty will choose how to integrate 3-D printers, tabletop CNC machines, laser cutters, and open-source micro controllers into studio education programs.

These pedagocial decisions are vital to students because they pertain to the choices that we are making in the present in relationship to our past and how we, as active agents in the present, are able to re-shape craft teaching and learning. If we look toward an unknown future from the viewpoint of tradition—the view that art history is likely to provide—we might anticipate the student's role is to become indoctrinated into the known and established working practices of craft. This approach views knowledge as external to the self and it holds up the canon from the historical view—a sense of craft tradition that ultimately must be learned, accepted, and abided by.

But yet, there is a frontier of craft knowledge in the present that upholds the primacy of the student's individual power and purpose. This approach to teaching and learning values the individual act of creation and represents a shift in emphasis toward the student's own development of knowledge or wisdom. It is a shift in focus and it involves placing more trust and autonomy in the aims of the student.

Today, we have choices to make in terms of "crafting a continuum." We can choose to use new technologies that empower our students to frame their own purposes. We can

trust in the student's own unique impulses rather than the certainty of our own canonical legacy from the historical view of craft. Therefore, to *rethink craft* is to choose an uncertain course that is necessary if we want a more progressive *craft*.

**Dennis Stevens** is a New York City-based visual artist, writer and media producer as well as a designer and developer of pedagogical strategies that use technology to engage online communities in educative conversations. His work can be found online at: www.beastsandlunatics.com, www.redefiningcraft.com, and www.vastplayground.com

## OBSERVATIONS ON CONTEMPORARY WORKS IN WOOD

by Christine Lee

Interwoven between the various disciplines of art, craft, design, and architecture, wood is a medium with an indelible and significant historical and contemporary presence. We are surrounded by sculptural, functional and structural work that reflects its inherent beauty, strength, and resilience. Experimentation with this versatile material has created a plethora of concepts and designs across a wide range of end-forms.

For some, computer-controlled machines, such as the CNC router and laser engraver, have become part of the tool set used to explore this material, but, personally, I find pieces generated entirely from this technology to be a bit sterile. A balance between technological advancements and the maker's hand creates the finest work: for example, the "PS2; Pattern Study Series," made by Jennifer Anderson (b. 1972), is a series of stools made from beech with through mortise-and-tenons cut by hand and patterns inspired by pleats in fabric cut with the CNC. Anderson values experimentation but also celebrates the therapeutic aspect of working with her hands. The stools exhibit solid wood surface exploration using the CNC, and at the same time, the process and importance of craft is evident in the hand-cut joinery and degree of finish in the final forms.

While highly crafted wood pieces that combine handwork and computer-aided technology are becoming more common, wood is also being used to create engaging installation forms, such as *Believing* by Yuri Kobayashi (b. 1971). Made from ash (with pieces over six feet tall), this installation must be assembled completely by hand and secured with sterling silver pins. Kobayashi believes in working directly with the material regardless of how much physical labor and handwork is involved. The expression of her idea involves pushing the structural limitations of the medium while engaging in extremely repetitive processes, which she identifies mostly with the assembly stage. Simultaneously she uses her hand tools to manipulate each wood element. Kobayashi's complex large-scale wood installation is dynamic—an exploration of the physical boundaries of the medium that is not meant to be permanently affixed or glued—and also elegant, in its form and high level of craftsmanship.

Anderson and Kobayashi represent the variety of individuals—old and young, formally trained or self-taught, emerging or established in practice—who continue to create compelling works in wood. Their trajectory began with formal education and training, continued with graduate studies in woodworking/furniture design, which propelled them onto a path of exploration that they continue to pursue. Their extensive experience with wood has allowed them to explore its inherent characteristics or push its limitations, while at the same time they remain connected to the process with direct material manipulation and commitment to craft. What seems evident in their work, and what is ultimately the criteria for engaging contemporary works in wood, is the pursuit of material exploration and experimentation balanced with a reverence for direct process and craft.

**Christine Lee** is an artist, designer, and researcher who integrates functional design and sculptural installation with discarded materials. Lee has exhibited in galleries and museums throughout the United States, including the Museum of Arts and Design in New York City, Aspen Art Museum, the Society for Contemporary Craft in Pittsburgh, and the San Francisco Museum of Craft and Design. Lee received a BFA from the University of Wisconsin-Madison and an MFA from San Diego State University.

# CHECKLIST

Works are listed in chronological order: height precedes width precedes depth.

## CERAMICS

1. Asger Jorn, Danish, 1914–1973
*Vessel*, 1953
Glazed ceramic
20¼ x 13 x 13 in.
Stéphane Janssen and R. Michael Johns Collection

2. Rudy Autio, American, 1926–2007
*Ceramic Pot*, 1966
Glazed stoneware, luster
16¼ x 12½ x 6½ in.
Purchased with funds provided by the American Art
Heritage Fund

3. Peter Voulkos, American, 1924–2002
*Steel Pot*, 1968
Glazed stoneware
32½ x 11½ x 11½ in.
Purchased with funds provided by the American Art
Heritage Fund

4. Marilyn Levine, Canadian, 1935–2005
*Dark Grey Satchel*, 1974
Earthenware, stains, luster
8⅝ x 14½ x 7⅜ in.
National Endowment for the Arts Matching Funds Grant

5. Marilyn Levine, Canadian, 1935–2005
*Eyelet Boots,* 1979
Earthenware, stains, leather laces
8¼ x 15¼ x 5 in.
Gift of Anne and Sam Davis

6. Betty Woodman, American, b. 1930
*Persian Pillow Pitcher*, 1980
Glazed earthenware
16¾ x 21⅝ x 12½ in.
Gift of Jay and Joyce Cooper

7. Robert Arneson, American, 1930–1992
*The Abstract Expressionist,* 1985
Glazed ceramic
34 x 26 x 10 in.
Stéphane Janssen and R. Michael Johns Collection
Art © Estate of Robert Arneson/Licensed by VAGA,
New York

8. Beatrice Wood, American, 1893–1998
*Untitled Teapot,* 1987
Glazed stoneware
18 x 19 x 10 in.
Stéphane Janssen and R. Michael Johns
Collection

9. Arman (Arman Fernandez),
American, born France, 1928–2005
*Demie Tasse*, 1990, 58/175
Glazed porcelain
Dimensions variable
Gift of the Helme Prinzen Estate

10. Akio Takamori, Japanese, active in
America, b. 1950
*Laocoön (Woman Reading)*, 1994
Glazed porcelain, overglaze
25 x 21½ x 9 in.
Gift of Anne and Sam Davis

11. Viola Frey, American, 1933–2004
*Possessions I*, 1996
Glazed ceramic
23 x 25 x 18 in.
Gift of Sara and David Lieberman
Art © Artists' Legacy Foundation/Licensed by
VAGA, New York

12. Beth Cavener Stichter, American, b. 1972
*Object Lesson: Apathy*, 2003
Stoneware, terra sigillata
27¼ x 30 x 22 in.
Diane and Sandy Besser Collection

13. Takashi Hinoda, Japanese, b. 1968
*Everyday War*, 2004
Glazed ceramic
21⁵⁄₁₆ x 11¹³⁄₁₆ x 10³⁄₁₆ in.
Purchased with funds provided by the Herbert
H. and Barbara C. Dow Foundation

14. Anders Ruhwald, Danish, b. 1974
*You Are Here, This Is It*, 2006
Glazed earthenware, painted steel, piping,
rubber caps
20 x 18 x 21 in.
Gift of the Artist

15. Anders Ruhwald, Danish, b. 1974
*Form and Function, #2*, 2006
Glazed earthenware, painted steel, piping, rubber caps
30 x 40 x 28 in.
Purchased with funds provided by the Windgate Charitable Foundation

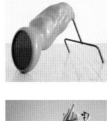

16. Louise Hindsgavl, Danish, b. 1973
*The Required Action*, 2010
Glazed porcelain, mixed media
25 x 27 x 16 in.
Anonymous Gift

17. Steen Ipsen, Danish, b. 1966
*Tied Up #62*, 2010
Glazed stoneware, cord
12 x 17½ x 10½ in.
Purchased with funds provided by the Windgate Charitable Foundation

18. Linda Sormin, Thai, b. 1971
*Wanli*, 2010
Glazed earthenware, found objects (metal ship, porcelain shards of dish by Sanam Emami)
20 x 22 x 23 in.
Purchased with funds provided by the Windgate Charitable Foundation

19. Huang Binyan, Chinese, b. 1984
*Rabbit #3*, 2011
Cast porcelain, overglaze
37½ x 12¾ x 9¾ in.
Gift of Anne and Sam Davis by exchange

20. CLAYDIES: Karen Kjældgård-Larsen, b. 1974 and Tine Broksø, b.1971, Danish
*True Feelings*, 2011
Glazed porcelain
Dimensions variable
Purchased with funds provided by the Windgate Charitable Foundation

21. Future Retrieval: Guy Michael Davis, b. 1979 and Katie Parker, b.1980, American
*Hye-Que Monkey in Captivity*, 2011
Glazed porcelain, screenprint, wood
54 x 24 x 7 in.
Purchased with funds provided by the Windgate Charitable Foundation

22. Gustaf Nordenskiöld, Swedish, b. 1966
Mure, 2011
Colored porcelain, rope
20 x 17½ x 10½ in.
Purchased with funds provided by the Windgate Charitable Foundation

23. Paul Scott, English, b. 1953
*Scott's Cumbrian Blue(s)- A Willow for Ai Weiwei, Wen Tao, Liu Zhenggang, Zhang Jinsong, Hu Mingfen*, 2011
Found object (porcelain, c. 1840), decals
8¹¹/₁₆ x 10⁵/₈ x 1³/₁₆ in.
Gift of the artist

24. Per B. Sundberg, Swedish, b. 1964
*The Gathering*, 2011
Glazed porcelain, found objects
11 x 9 x 9 in.
Purchased with funds provided by the Windgate Charitable Foundation

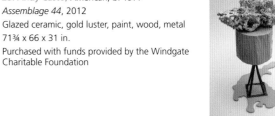

25. Andy Casto, American, b. 1977
*Assemblage 44*, 2012
Glazed ceramic, gold luster, paint, wood, metal
71¾ x 66 x 31 in.
Purchased with funds provided by the Windgate Charitable Foundation

26. Mia Göransson, Swedish, b. 1961
*Squares of Nature*, 2012
Glazed porcelain
36 x 36 x 3 in.
Purchased with funds provided by the Windgate Charitable Foundation

27. Del Harrow, American, b. 1977
*Cabinet #3*, 2012
Porcelain, luster, wood
30 x 60 x 24 in.
Purchased with funds provided by the Windgate Charitable Foundation

28. David Hicks, American, b. 1977
*Flora* (yellow melt), 2012
Glazed terracotta
24 x 15 x 14 in.
Gift of the Artist

29. Karin Karinson Nilsson, Swedish, b. 1970
*This Was Not a Sneak Attack*, 2012
Glazed porcelain, glass, mixed media
13 x 13½ x 10½ in.
Purchased with funds provided by the Windgate Charitable Foundation

# WOOD

30. Tom Eckert, American, b. 1942
*MM-342 (Tank Chair)*, 1980
Hard maple
34½ x 30½ x 36 in.
Gift of E. Tom and Erika Meyer

31. Mark Lindquist, American, b. 1949
*Unsung Bowl #1*, 1981
Cherry burl
9¾ x 10¹¹/₁₆ x 10 in.
Gift of Edward Jacobson

32. David Ellsworth, American, b. 1944
*Emerald Moon*, 1982
Lignum vitae
9½ x 7¼ x 7¼ in.
Gift of Edward Jacobson

33. Stephen Hogbin, British, resides in Canada, b. 1942
*Walking Bowl*, 1983
Zebrawood
10⁷/₈ x 6⁷/₈ x 8¼ in.
Gift of Edward Jacobson

34. Ed Moulthrop, American, 1916–2003
*Vessel*, 1990
Cedar
25³/₈ x 19 x 19 in.
Gift of the artist and The Hand and The Spirit

35. Virginia Dotson, American, b. 1943
*Wind Eye Series, #1*, 1992
Marfim plywood, plexiglass
12¼ x 8½ x 8½ in.
Gift of the Artist

36. Philip Moulthrop, American, b. 1947
*White Pine Mosaic Bowl*, 1992
White pine, epoxy
15⁷/₈ x 18 x 18 in.
Purchased with funds provided by the American Art Heritage Fund

37. Todd Hoyer, American, b. 1952
*Ringed Series*, 1997
Cottonwood, wire
9 x 15 x 15 in.
Gift of Sara and David Lieberman

38. Connie Mississippi, American, b. 1941
*Evening Stillness*, 2000
Laminated Baltic birch plywood, paint
8 x 22 x 22 in.
Gift of Robyn and John Horn

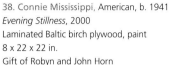

39. Robyn Horn, American, b. 1951
*Token Stone* from the *Slipping Stone* Series, 2003
Red gum burl
16½ x 18 x 6 in.
Purchased with funds provided by the Herbert H. and Barbara C. Dow Foundation

40. Howard Werner, American, b. 1951
*Poplar Vessel*, 2003
Poplar
56 x 38 x 15¼ in.
Museum Purchase with funds provided by the Windgate Charitable Foundation

41. Claudette Schreuders, South African, b. 1973
*New Shoes*, 2003–2004
Jacaranda wood, enamel paint
30½ x 12 x 9¾ in.
Museum purchase with funds provided by the Windgate Charitable Foundation

42. Efrain Almeida, Brazilian, b. 1964
Untitled, 2004
Cedar, plastic beads
60 x 48 x 5 in.
Museum purchase with funds provided by the Windgate Charitable Foundation

43. Yoshimasa Tsuchiya, Japanese, b. 1977
*Carnival*, 2005
Hinoki (Japanese cypress), paint, crystals
6 x 11 x 8 in.
Purchased with funds provided by the Windgate Charitable Foundation

44. Alison Elizabeth Taylor, American, b. 1973
*Chainlink*, 2008
Wood veneer, shellac
34 x 46 x 1 in.
Purchased with funds provided by the
 Windgate Charitable Foundation

45.Katie Hudnall, American, b. 1979
*Bolt Reliquary*, 2011
Recycled wood, mixed media
62 x 40 x 15 in.
Purchased with funds provided by the
Windgate Charitable Foundation

46. Marc Ricourt, French, b. 1963
*Lime Wood Sculpture,* 2011
Lime wood, oxide
7¼ x 13½ x 12 in.
Purchased with funds provided by the
Windgate Charitable Foundation

47.David Rowe, American, b. 1982
Untitled, 2011
Recycled wood,
mixed media
40 x 140 x 20 in.
Purchased with
funds provided by the
Windgate Charitable Foundation

48. Matthias Pliessnig, American, b. 1978
*Brace*, 2012
White oak, copper
17 x 88 x 39 in.
Commissioned with funds by the
Windgate Charitable Foundation

# FIBER

49. Ed Rossbach, American, 1914–2002
*Pete Rose*, 1982
Folded newspaper strips, paint
6¾ x 6¾ x 6⅞ in.
Purchased with funds provided by the ASU Art
Museum Store

50. Ed Rossbach, American,1914–2002
*Japanese Plaited Basket*, 1987
Stapled rag paper
11½ x 12 x 12 in.
Gift of Janet and Roger Robinson

51. Joanne Segal Brandford, American,
1933–1994
*Basket-figure,* 1983
Fiber
15½ x 13³/₈ x 4¾ in.
Diane and Sandy Besser Collection

52. Lillian Elliott, American, 1930–1994
*Shaped Bark*, 1991
Bark, linen
10 x 22 x 20 in.
Gift of Sara and David Lieberman

53. Lillian Elliott, American, 1930–1994
Pat Hickman, American, b. 1941
*Walk in the Woods*, 1986
Hog gut, sticks
16 x 9 x 9 in.
Gift of Janet and Roger Robinson

54. Dorothy Gill Barnes, American, b. 1927
*Coiled Banyan*, 1988
Banyan
7 x 25 x 25 in.
Diane and Sandy Besser Collection

55. John Garrett, American, b. 1950
*Triumph*, 1991
Copper, glass beads
14½ x 19 x 19 in.
Diane and Sandy Besser Collection

56. John McQueen, American, b. 1943
*CULTIVAR* "a tree can't but be," 1992
Plywood, screws
60 x 24 x 27 in.
Gift of Sara and David Lieberman

57. Kay Sekimachi, American, b. 1926
*Washi Vessel*, c. 1995
Antique Japanese paper, folded and machine stitched
22 x 6 x 6 in.
Gift of Sara and David Lieberman

58. Jerry Bleem, American, b. 1954
*Weight/Wait*, 1998
Business cards, wax, acrylic medium, staples, stone
6½ x 12¼ x 5 in.
Gift of the Artist

59. Ferne Jacobs, American, b. 1942
*Tides*, 2003
Waxed linen thread
26 x 17 x 17 in.
Promised gift of Sara and David Lieberman

60. Gyöngy Laky, Hungarian, resides in the United States, b. 1944
*Linkage*, 2005
Manzanita, red ink, metal screws
46 x 47 x 4½ in.
Promised gift of Sara and David Lieberman

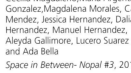
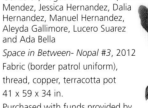

61. Lisa Telford, American (Haida), b. 1957
*Moon Warrior*, 2005
Red cedar bark, cordage, abalone buttons
25 x 14 x 9 in.
Promised gift of Sara and David Lieberman

62. Leon Niehues, American, b. 1951
*Warrior*, 2009
Oak strips, emery cloth, metal rivets
16 x 13 x 13 in.
Gift of Robyn and John Horn

63. Jarbas Lopes, Brazilian, b. 1964
*Cicloviaéra*, 2006
Oisier (natural fiber vine) over bicycle
42 x 72 x 20½ in.
Purchased with funds provided by the
Herbert H. and Barbara C. Dow Foundation

64. Mark Newport, American, b. 1964
*W Man*, 2009
Hand-knit acrylic, buttons
80 x 23 x 6 in.
Purchased with funds provided by the Windgate
Charitable Foundation

65. Mark Newport, American, b. 1964
*Two Gun Kid*, 2006
Embroidered comic book cover
11 x 7 in.
Purchased with funds provided by the
Windgate Charitable Foundation

66. Sonya Clark, American, b. 1967
*Threadwrapped in Blue and Brown*, 2008
Combs, thread
60 x 45 x 1 in.
Purchased with funds provided by the
Windgate Charitable Foundation

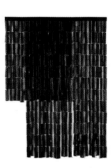

67. Margarita Cabrera, Mexican, b. 1973
In collaboration with: Flor Garcia, Ana Patricia,
Magda Vazquez, Rocio Magdaleno, Narfdaf Aponte,
Cecilia Magdaleno,Maria Argentina Reyes, Yanira
Gonzalez,Magdalena Morales, Caritinia Vega, Liliana
Mendez, Jessica Hernandez, Dalia
Hernandez, Manuel Hernandez,
Aleyda Gallimore, Lucero Suarez
and Ada Bella
*Space in Between- Nopal #3*, 2012
Fabric (border patrol uniform),
thread, copper, terracotta pot
41 x 59 x 34 in.
Purchased with funds provided by
the Windgate Charitable Foundation

68. Carol Eckert, American, b. 1945
*And a Wolf Shall Devour the Sun*, 2012
Black waxed linen thread, wire
14 x 65 x 3 in.
Anonymous Gift

# BIBLIOGRAPHY

## SUGGESTED READINGS

Adamson, Glenn. *The Craft Reader.* Oxford and New York: Berg, 2010.

_____. *Thinking Through Craft.* Oxford and New York: Berg, 2007.

Adamson, Glenn, and Jane Pavitt. *Post Modernism: Style and Subversion, 1970–1990.* London: V&A Publishing, 2011.

Alfoldy, Sandra, ed. *Neo Craft: Modernity and the Crafts.* Halifax, NS: The Press of the Nova Scotia College of Art and Design, 2007.

Auter, Elissa. String, *Felt, and the Hierarchy of Art and Craft in American Art, 1960–1980.* Minneapolis: University of Minnesota Press, 2009.

Bell, Nicholas. *40 under 40: Craft Futures.* Washington, DC, and New Haven, CT: Smithsonian American Art Museum and Yale University Press, 2012

_____. *A Revolution in Wood: The Bresler Collection.* Washington, DC: Smithsonian American Art Museum, 2011.

Burgard, Timothy Anglin, Karin Breuer, and Jill D' Alessandron. *The Diane and Sandy Besser Collection.* San Francisco: Fine Arts Museums of San Francisco, 2007.

Buszek, Maria Elena, ed. *Extra/Ordinary: Craft and Contemporary Art.* Durham, NC: Duke University Press, 2011.

Butcher, Mary, ed. *Contemporary International Basketmaking.* London: Merell Holberton, 1999.

Clark, Garth. *Anne Davis Collection: Contemporary British and American Clay.* El Paso, TX: El Paso Museum of Art, 1993.

Clark, Garth, ed. *Ceramic Millennium: Critical Writings on Ceramic History, Theory, and Art.* Halifax, N.S.: Press of the Nova Scotia College of Art and Design, 2006.

Clark, Garth, and Cindi Strauss. *Shifting Paradigms in Contemporary Ceramics: The Garth Clark and Mark Del Vecchio Collection.* Houston and New Haven, CT: Museum of Fine Arts, Houston, and Yale University Press, 2012.

Collins, Jane L. *Threads: Gender, Labor, and Power in the Global Apparel Industry.* Chicago: The University of Chicago Press, 2003.

Crawford, Matthew. *Shop Class as Soul Craft: An Inquiry into the Value of Work.* New York: Penguin Press, 2009.

De Waal, Edmund. *20th Century Ceramics.* London: Thames & Hudson, 2003.

De Waal, Edmund, and Claudia Clare. *The Pot Book.* London and New York: Phaidon, 2011.

Del Vecchio, Mark. *Postmodern Ceramics.* New York: Thames & Hudson, 2001.

Dietz, Ulysses Grant. *Great Pots: Contemporary Ceramics from Function to Form.* Madison, WI: Guild Publishing, 2003.

Dormer, Peter, ed. *The Culture of Craft: Status and Future.* New York: Manchester University Press, 1997.

Douglas, Mary F., et al. *Allan Chasanoff Ceramic Collection.* Charlotte, NC: Mint Museum of Craft and Design, 2000.

*Expressions in Wood: Masterworks From The Wornick Collection.* Oakland: Oakland Museum of California, 1996.

Fariello, Anna M., and Paula Owen, eds. *Objects and Meaning: New Perspectives on Art and Craft.* Maryland: Scarecrow Press, 2004.

Foster, Hal. *Design and Crime: and Other Diatribes.* London: Verso, 2002.

Greenhalgh, Paul, ed. *The Persistence of Craft: The Applied Arts Today.* New Brunswick, NJ: Rutgers University Press, 2003.

Hampton, Monica, and Lily Kane. *Shaping the Future of Craft.* New York: American Craft Council, 2007.

Hapler, Vicki, and Diane Douglas, eds. *Choosing Craft: The Artist's Viewpoint.* Chapel Hill: University of North Carolina Press, 2009.

Hecht, Ann. *The Art of the Loom: Weaving, Spinning, and Dyeing Across the World.* Seattle: University of Washington Press, 2001.

Held, Peter, et al. *A Ceramic Continuum: Fifty Years of the Archie Bray Influence.* Helena, MT, and Seattle: Holter Museum of Art and University of Washington Press, 2001.

Herman, Lloyd. The *Collector's Eye: Contemporary Ceramics American, Canadian, and British from the Collection of Aaron Mildred.* Ontario, Canada: Koffler Center of the Arts, 1994.

Hogbin, Stephen. *Appearance and Reality: A Visual Handbook for Artists, Designers and Makers.* Bethel, CT: Cambium Press, 2000.

Jacobson, Edward. *The Art of Turned-wood Bowls.* New York: E.P. Dutton, 1985.

Jönsson, Love. *Craft in Dialogue: Six Views on a Practice in Change.* Stockholm: International Artists' Studio Program in Sweden, 2005.

Lauria, Jo, and Steve Fenton. *Craft in America: Celebrating Two Centuries of Artists and Objects.* New York: Clarkson Potter, 2007.

Lauria, Jo, et al. *Color and Fire: Defining Moments in Studio Ceramics, 1950–2000.* Los Angeles: Los Angeles County Museum of Art, 1990.

Levine, Faythe, and Cortney Heimerl, eds. *Handmade Nation: The Rise of DIY, Art, Craft, and Design.* New York: Princeton Architectural Press, 2008.

Livingstone, Joan, and John Ploof, eds. *The Object of Labor: Art, Cloth, and Cultural Production* (anthology). Cambridge, MA: MIT Press, 2007.

*Living with Form: The Horn Collection of Contemporary Crafts.* Little Rock: Arkansas Arts Center and Bradley Publishing, 1999.

Lynn, Martha Drexler. *Clay Today, Contemporary Ceramists and Their Work.* Los Angeles: Los Angeles County Museum of Art, 1990.

Martin, Terry, and Kevin Wallace. *New Masters of Woodturning: Expanding the Boundaries of Wood Art.* East Petersburg, PA: Fox Chapel Publishing, 2008.

McFadden, David Revere. *Radical Lace and Subversive Knitting.* New York: Museum of Art and Design, 2007.

Molesworth, Helen. *Work Ethic.* Philadelphia: Pennsylvania State University Press, 2003.

Murray, Kevin. Craft *Unbound: Make the Common Precious.* Port Melbourne: Thames and Hudson Australia, 2005.

Newell, Laurie Britton. *Out of the Ordinary: Spectacular Craft.* London: V&A Publications, 2007.

Oakes, Kaya. *Slanted and Enchanted: The Evolution of Indie Culture.* New York: Holt Paperbacks, 2009.

Perry, Barbara, et al. *American Ceramics: The Collection of the Everson Museum of Art.* New York: Rizzoli International Publications, 1989.

Peterson, Susan. *Contemporary Ceramics.* New York: Watson-Guptil Publications, 2000.

Ramljak, Suzanne, and Michael Monroe. *Turning Wood into Art: The Jane and Arthur Mason Collection.* Charlotte, NC: Mint Museum of Craft and Design, 2000.

Randall, Judson, ed. *Connections: International Turning Exchange 1995–2005.* Philadelphia: The Center For Art in Wood, 2005.

Risatti, Howard. *A Theory of Craft: Function and Aesthetic Expression.* Chapel Hill: University of North Carolina Press, 2007.

Sennet, Richard. *The Craftsman.* New Haven, CT: Yale University Press, 2008.

Sims, Lowry. *Against the Grain: Wood in Contemporary Art, Craft and Design.* New York: Museum of Art and Design and the Monacelli Press, 2012.

Sövik, Elisabeth, ed. *Conversations With Wood: The Collection of Ruth and David Waterbury.* Minneapolis: Minneapolis Institute of Arts, 2011.

*Textile Society of America Symposium Proceedings.* http://digitalcommons.unl.edu/tsaconf/

Walsh, Penny. *The Yarn Book.* Philadelphia: University of Pennsylvania Press, 2006.

Ward, Gerald, and Julie Muniz. *She Boy, She Devil, and Isis: the Art of Conceptual Craft.* Boston: MFA Publications, 2007.

Watson, Oliver. *Studio Pottery: Twentieth-century British Ceramics in the Victoria and Albert Museum Collection.* London: Victoria and Albert Museum and Phaidon Press, 1993.

*Wood Turning in North America Since 1930.* Philadelphia and New Haven, CT: The Center For Art In Wood and Yale University Art Gallery, 2003.

## ASUAM CRAFT PUBLICATIONS

*by date*

*Fiber Concepts*, 1989. Introduction by Lucinda H. Gedeon. 24 pp.

*Selections from the Joyce and Jay Cooper Collection of Contemporary Ceramics*, 1989. Introduction by Lucinda H. Gedeon. 8 pp.

*Turned Wood Now: Redefining the Lathe-Turned Objects, IV*, 1997. Essays by Heather Sealy Lineberry and John Perreault.

64 pp.

*Shared Passion: Sara and David Lieberman Collection of Contemporary Ceramics and Craft*, 2003. Foreword by Dean J. Roberts Wills. Essays by Peter Held and Susan Peterson. Catalogue includes a DVD interview with Sara and David Lieberman. 48 pp., DVD approx 25 min.

*Humor, Irony and Wit: Ceramic Funk from the Sixties and Beyond*, 2004. Foreword by Peter Held. Interview between Peter Held and Jay Cooper. Essays by John Natsoulas and Rick Newby. 48 pp.

*The Long Day: Sculpture by Claudette Schreuders*, 2004. Foreword by Marilyn A. Zeitlin. Essays by Heather Sealy Lineberry and Tina Yapelli. 40 pp.

*Intertwined: Contemporary Baskets from the Sara and David Lieberman Collection*, 2005. Foreword by Marilyn A. Zeitlin. Essays by Kenneth R. Trapp and Ferne Jacobs. Introduction by Heather Sealy Lineberry. 48 pp.

*Between Clouds of Memory: Akio Takamori, A Mid-career Survey*, 2005. Foreword by Marilyn A. Zeitlin. Essays by Peter Held, Edward Lebow, and Toyojiro Hida. 156 pp. (English and Japanese).

*Mark Newport: Super Heroics*, 2005. Foreword by Marilyn A. Zeitlin. Essay by John D. Spiak. 24 pp.

*A Ceramic Legacy: The Stéphane Janssen and R. Michael Johns Collection*, 2006. Foreword by Marilyn A. Zeitlin. Essay by Peter Held. Text by R. Michael Johns and Ralph Bacerra. 22 pp.

*Everyday Miracles: Latin American Folk Art from the Cecere Collection*, 2007. Foreword by Marilyn Zeitlin. Essay by Joanne Stuhr. 32 pp.

*Moulthrop Generations: Turned Wood Bowls by Ed, Philip, and Matt Moulthrop*, 2007. Foreword by Marilyn A. Zeitlin. Essays by Joanne Rapp and Heather Sealy Lineberry. 40 pp.

*Following the Rhythms of Life: The Ceramic Art of David Shaner*, 2007. Foreword by Marilyn Zeitlin. Introduction by Peter Held. Essays by Jack Troy and Peter Held with contributions by Conan Putnam and Hollis Walker. 120 pp.

*Eden Revisited: The Ceramic Art of Kurt Weiser*, 2008. Foreword by Dean Kwang-Wu Kim. Introduction by Peter Held. Essays by Ulysses Grant Dietz, Peter Held and Edward Lebow. 120 pp.

*A Human Impulse: Figuration from the Diane and Sandy Besser Collection*, 2008. Introduction by Peter Held. Interview between Peter Held and Sandy Besser. Essay by Kate Bonansinga. 96 pp.

*Susan Beiner: Synthetic Reality*, 2008. Introduction by Peter Held. Essay by Kathleen Vanesian. 24 pp.

*Innovation and Change: Ceramics From the Arizona State University Art Museum*, 2009. Foreword by Dean Kwang-Wu Kim. Introduction by Peter Held. Essays by Heather Sealy Lineberry and Peter Held with Germaine Shames. 224 pp.

*A Chosen Path: The Ceramic Art of Karen Karnes*, 2010. Foreword by Garth Clark. Curator's Statement by Peter Held. Introduction by Mark Shapiro. Essays by Christopher Benfry, Jody Clowes, Janet Koplos, Edward Lebow and Karen Karnes. 174pp.

*Infinite Place: The Ceramic Art of Wayne Higby*, 2013. Foreword by Helen W. Drutt English. Essays by Carla Coch, Tanya Harrod, Peter Held, Wayne Higby, Mary Drach McInnes, Henry Sayre and Ezra Shales. 216 pp.

# ASU ADMINISTRATION AND STAFF

## ADMINISTRATION

### ARIZONA STATE UNIVERSITY

Michael M. Crow, *President*
Elizabeth D. Phillips, *Executive Vice President and Provost of the University*

### HERBERGER INSTITUTE FOR DESIGN AND THE ARTS

Kwang-Wu Kim, *Dean and Director*
Heather Landes, *Associate Dean*
Patrick Smith, *Assistant Dean*
Michael Underhill, *Executive Dean*
Shawn Richards, *Director of Development*

### ADVISORY BOARD

Peter Shikany, *Chair*
Dorina Bustamante
Sherry Cameron
Dan Fairris
Scott Jarson
William F. Joffroy, Jr.
Eddie Jones
Eric Jungermann
Braden Kay
Jon Kitchell
Greg Lehmann
Michael Martin
Sloane McFarland
Katy Owens
Louise Roman
Eddie Shea
Ridge Smidt
Eileen Spitalny
David Villadolid

Gordon Knox, *ex officio*
Heather Sealy Lineberry, *ex officio*

### ARTISTS' ADVISORY COMMITTEE, CERAMICS RESEARCH CENTER

Char Applen
Tiffany Bailey
Barbara Baskerville
Sarah Brodie
Tom Budzak
Stephen Bunyard
Jeanne Collins
Paulette Galop
James Gamble
Lisa Harnish
Haldor Hjalmarson
Linda Painter
Kelly O'Briant
Genie Swanstrom
Greg Wenz

## ARIZONA STATE UNIVERSITY ART MUSEUM STAFF

Gordon Knox, *Director*
Heather Sealy Lineberry, *Associate Director and Senior Curator*
Felix Aguirre, *Visitor Services Coordinator*
Robert Bargman, *Security Officer/ Visitor Services*
Michael Brennan, *Lead Security Officer*
Mary-Beth Buesgen, *Program Specialist, Ceramics Research Center*
Stacy Chatham, *Administrative Associate to the Director*
Vanessa Piso Cornwall, *Business Specialist*
Gregory Esser, *Associate Director, Desert Initiative*
Andrea Feller, *Curator of Education*
Elisa Benavidez Hayes, *Assistant Registrar*
Peter Held, *Curator of Ceramics*
Nicole Herden, *Curatorial Assistant and Windgate Curatorial Intern*
Stephen Johnson, *Chief Preparator*
Elizabeth Johnson, *HIDA Coordinator, Socially Engaged Practice*
Leila Kelly, *Registrar Assistant*
Elizabeth Kozlowski, *Windgate Curatorial Fellow*
Aimee León, *Curatorial Intern*
Janis Munsil, *Museum Store Specialist*
Jean Makin, *Print Collection Manager/ Curator*
Christopher Miller, *Assistant Preparator*
Julio Cesar Morales, *Curator*
Jason Ripper, *Security Officer/ Visitor Services*
Eduardo Rivera, *Security Officer/ Visitor Services*
Anne Sullivan, *Registrar*
Deborah Susser, *Publicist*

## CERAMIC LEADERS AT ASU

(as of May 31, 2013)

### PATRON MEMBERS

Anonymous
Artists' Advisory Committee, Ceramics Research Center
Patricia and Frank AtLee
Masako and Ron Berman
David Charak
Elaine and Sidney Cohen
Anne and Sam Davis
Jo and Ronald Davis
Patrick Doust and Richard North
Mary Fisher and Family
Carol and Edward Hall
Stéphane Janssen
Sara and David Lieberman
Joan and David Lincoln
Janet and Roger Robinson
Merle and Steve Rosskam
Mindy and Michael Solomon
Jeffrey Spahn
Nancy Tieken
Trudy and Steven Wiesenberger
Kurt and Christy Weiser

### CONTRIBUTING MEMBERS

Judy Ackerman and Richard Epstein
Lyndall Eddy and Phillip Wagoner
Midge and Jerry Golner
Sally and Richard Lehman
Josefine and David Perry
Joanne and James Rapp
Arlene and Mort Scult

### SUPPORTING MEMBERS

Debbie and Robert Burger
Janet Orr
Vivian Rae Spiegelman and Edward Lebow
Wanda Turk

### ACTIVE MEMBERS

Stephen Alpert
Char Applen
Linda and James Ballinger
Maureen and John Chestnut
Joyce Cooper
William Daley
Sharon and Paul Dauer
Emily and Fred Gurtman
Roberta and Bruce Hammer
Marian Hieda
Linda Sheppard and John Hill
Ann and Keith Kelly
Judith Mathis
Diane and Carleton Moore

Deanna and John O'Donnell
Joan Prior and John Armstrong
Jan Schachter
Christy Vezolles
Ruth and Robert Vogele
Patti Warashina
Mikki and Stanley Weithorn

### INDIVIDUAL MEMBERS

Ben Gordon
Suzanne and Stuart Rutkin
Jill Seymour
Elizabeth and George Woodman

## FRIENDS OF THE ASU ART MUSEUM

(as of May 31, 2013)

### PATRON MEMBERS

Jean and Harold Grossman

### CONTRIBUTING MEMBERS

Merle and Steve Rosskam
Masako and Ronald Berman

### SUPPORTING MEMBERS

Maureen and John Chestnut
Carol Christine
Joyce Cooper
Rita and Richard Goldberg
Richard Goldsmith
Midge and Gerald Golner
Erik Hemp
John Hill and Linda Sheppard

Bonita and Russell Nelson
Craig Pearson
Joseph Pizzicaroli
Joanne and James Rapp
Carolyn and Philip Robins
Laura and Herb Roskind
Barbara and Donald Tober
Gai Williams
Phillip Wagoner and Lyndall Eddy
Christy Vezolles

### ACTIVE MEMEBERS

Lisa Alexander
Marie Allison
Betsy Fahlman-Ball and Dan Ball
Alice and Ron Bimrose
Dr. Claudia Brown and Dr. Richard Stevenson
Penelope Cagney
Peggy Cash
Dr. Barbara and Lem Cortright
Shirley Curran
Geny Dignac

Karyn Gitlis and Philip Douglass
Carol and Thomas Eckert
Mary Erickson
Susan Felt
Sandra Ferniza
Marvin Fisher
Edith and Morris Frieband
Pamela Garrett
Dr. Susan Gray and Dr. John Gilkeson
Debra and Luke Glynn
Ben Gordon
Emily and Fred Gurtman
Carol and Edward Hall
Diane Harrison and Dr. Sherman Axel
Rene Herrera
Dr. Ruth Jones
Ruby Kaufman
Charlotte and Norwin Landay
Patricia LaCrosse
Maxine and Dr. Ronald Linde
Emily Matyas and Mark Klett
Jodi and Michael Maas
Raimonde and Richard Manch
Jane and Douglas Metzger
Stuart Mitnik
Cynthia and Anthony Peterson
Jeanne Porter
Linda and Charles Redman
Nancy Robinson
Jo Rose
Gayle Shanks
Frank Skinner
Susan Soroka and David Spencer
David Spencer
Deanna Stulgaitis
Selma and Jerome Targovnik
Mollie Trivers and Shelley Cohn
Lynn Tulis
Bill VanOrden & Earla Marshall
Mikki and Stanley Weithorn
Mary (Kotzie) Wheeler
Edward Wong
Josseline and Rob Wood

## COMMUNITY INVESTORS

(as of May 31, 2013)

Windgate Charitable Foundation
Stéphane Janssen
Joan and David Lincoln

The Annenberg Foundation
Arizona Community Foundation
Arizona Home Care
Artists' Advisory Committee, Ceramics Research Center
Beavers Charitable Trust
City of Tempe
Erie Art Museum
Zalec Familian and Lilian Levinson Foundation
Friends of Contemporary Ceramics
Bill and Melinda Gates Foundation
Elizabeth Firestone Graham Foundation
The Harold and Jean Grossman Family Foundation
Diane and Bruce Halle Foundation
Hirsch Family Foundation
The Japan Foundation
King Galleries, Scottsdale, AZ
Marlin Miller Jr. Family Foundation
National Endowment for the Arts
The Lovena Ohl Foundation
The Steele Foundation, Inc.
Target
The Andy Warhol Foundation for the Visual Arts

David Ables
Alfred University
Stephen Alpert
Anonymous
Ant Farm
Ardagh Designs LTD.
Arizona Home Care
As You Wish Pottery
Hope Barkan
Sandra J. Blain
Rachel and Gerald Blank
Barry Brendan
Dorina Bustamante
Sherry Cameron
Sean Caulfield
Elaine and Sidney Cohen
Jenna Cooper
Joyce K. Cooper
Paula and Neil Cooperrider
Jo and Ron Davis
Sharon and Paul Dauer
Mark Del Vecchio and Garth Clark
Leatrice and Melvin Eagle
Carol and Tom Eckert
Lyndall Eddy and Phillip Wagoner

Susan Ellerin
Dan Fairris
Skippy and Emanuel Gerard
George Gibbons
Mimi and Sherman Gleeke
Midge and Jerry Golner
Diane and Marc Grainer
Emily and Fred Gurtman
Carl and Edward Hall
Diane and Bruce Halle
David Hicks
Wayne Higby
Robyn and John Horn
Laurie and George Jackson
Jason Jacques Gallery
Deborah and Scott Jarson
William Joffroy, Jr.
Darien Johnson
Eddie Jones
Edda Jonsdottir
Eric Jungermann
Braden Kay
Janice Kerr
Gretchen Keyworth
Leatrice and Jon Kitchell
Lucy Lacoste
Margo and Robert Lathrop
Greg Lehmann
Lewis and Clark College
Sara and David Lieberman
Steffen Lipofsky
Kate Lydon
Edward Marks
Grace and Paul Markovits
Michael Martin
Sloane McFarland
Ana Almeida and James Melikian
Network for Good
Michaela Orstav
Katy Owens
P.S. Studios, Inc.
Christine Pillsbury
Carlos Enrique Prado
Sue and Bernie Pucker
Martha Rieger
Janet and Roger Robinson
Louise Roman
Merle and Steve Rosskam
Anders Ruhwald
Anne Sanchez
Dr. Zeborah Schachtel
Paul Scott
Arlene and Mort Scult
Lisa Sette
Eddie Shea.
Peter Shikany
Sondra and Marvin Smalley
Tara and Ridge Smidt
Mindy and Michael Solomon

Mindy Solomon Gallery
Jeffrey Spahn Gallery
Eileen and Michael Spitalny
Donna and Howard Stone
Linda Lee Switzer
Maurine and Lawrence Taubman
Nancy Tieken
David Villadolid
Mikki and Stanley Weithorn
Trudy and Steven Wiesenberger
Gai L. Williams
Josseline and Rob Wood

# INDEX

# WE ARE NEW HERE

## BUTTE GODS AND CACTUS SAINTS

Works in progress by Windgate Artist-in-residence Nao Matsunaga, 2012.

What struck me most when we arrived in Arizona was the horizontalness of the built environment.

Looking out of a windshield, everything seemed to be stretched out sideways.

Sky was pushing everything down flat.

My sense of scale has been altered. I have always been fascinated by architectural models and georamas. There is a magical quality when one imagines oneself to be one inch tall and is able to explore these miniature spaces. It is an odd feeling to have this sensation as real life experience. This is exactly how I felt walking in downtown Phoenix on the weekend when we first arrived from London, standing in the middle of Monument Valley and catching my first glimpse of Grand Canyon.

Here, the sky and sunshine is something physical, tangible, with weight to it.

Here, human traces are new, the land so old. We are new here.

—Nao Matsunaga, March 2013

# PHOTO CREDITS

Key

ASUAM: Arizona State University Art Museum

ASUAM SHP Archive: Arizona State University Art Museum
Susan Harnly Peterson Archives

All photography by Craig Smith unless otherwise noted

Introduction
Pg. 8: Taylor Dabney
Pg. 10: ASUAM

Preface
Pg. 11: ASUAM (top left); Ken Howie Studios
(bottom left)
Pg. 12: ASUAM (top right, middle); Bob Rink
(bottom right)
Pg. 13: Daniel Swadener (top left); Peter Held (bottom left)
Pg. 14: Daniel Swadener

Thrown Off Center
Pg. 15: Magda Sayeg (top right); Courtesy of the
artist and Salon 94 Gallery, New York (bottom left)
Pg. 16: Bill Steen (top right); Peter Held (right
center); Courtesy of We Work In A Fragile Material
(bottom)
Pg. 17: Morgan Morell (top right)
Pg. 18: Mia Göransson (middle right)

From Studio Craft to Hybrid Practice
Pg. 21: Elizabeth Kozlowski (top left); ASUAM
(bottom left)
Pg. 22: Daniel Swadener (top right); ASUAM
(bottom right)
Pg. 23: Elizabeth Kozlowski (top left); Katie Hudnall
(bottom left); Courtesy of Margarita Cabrera
(bottom right)
Pg. 24: Tim Trumble

Craft-In-Residence
Pg. 25: Courtesy of Archie Bray Foundation for the
Ceramic Arts
Pg. 26: ASUAM SHP Archive
Pg. 27: Courtesy of Pottery Northwest (top left);
Courtesy of Arrowmont School of Arts and Crafts
Archives (bottom left)
Pg. 28: Andy Casto (bottom right)

The Time of the Object
Pg. 30: From The Huffington Post, 9/5/2012, © 2013
AOL Inc. All rights reserved. Used by permission
and protected by the Copyright Laws of the United
States. The printing, copying, redistribution, or re-
transmission of this Content without express written
permission is prohibited.
Pg. 31: Courtesy of the artists (top right); Courtesy
of Sundaram Tagore Gallery, New York, (bottom left)
Pg. 32: Ralph Esposito
Pg. 33: Tony Cuñha
Pg. 34: Magda Sayeg

Selected Works
Courtesy of the artist: pgs. 36, 91, 132, 151, 160-161
Taylor Dabney: pg. 163
Tom Grotta: 153
Don Nibert: 157

Søren Nielsen: Pgs. 62–63
Bruce Peterson: 155

Artist Portraits
Almeida: Courtesy of Ida Feldman
Arneson: ASU Art Museum, Studio Potter Archives,
Art © Estate of Robert Arneson/Licensed by VAGA,
New York, NY
Autio: Chris Autio
Barnes: Cory Piehowicz
Binyan: Courtesy of Lisa Sette Gallery
Bleem: Tom Van Eynde
Brandford: Paul Brandford
Cabrera: Melody Parra
Casto: Courtesy of the artist
Clark: Taylor Dabney
CLAYDIES: Anne Mie Drevers
Davis: Katie Parker
Dotson: Virginia David Barr
Eckert, C: Courtesy of the artist
Eckert, T: Courtesy of the artist
Elliott and Hickman: Paul Smith
Ellsworth: Courtesy of the artist
Fernandez: Images courtesy of the Arman Studio
Archives New York, NY
Frey: Courtesy American Craft Council, Art ©
Artists' Legacy Foundation/Licensed by VAGA,
New York, NY
Garrett: Margot Geist
Göransson: Courtesy of the artist
Harrow: Sanam Emami
Hicks: Courtesy of the artist
Hindsgavl: Anne Mie Dreves
Hinoda: Courtesy of the artist
Hogbin: Michael McLuhan
Horn: Matt Bradley
Hoyer: Hayley Smith
Hudnall: Michelle Given
Ipsen: Ole Akhoej
Jacobs: Courtesy of Nancy Margolis Gallery, 2013
Jorn: Museum Jorn, Denmark. Johs Jensen, pho-
tographer
Laky: Lucia Zegada
Levine: ASU Art Museum Studio Potter Archives
Lindquist: Spencer Bennett / © Lindquist Studios,
all rights reserved.
Lopes: Courtesy of the artist
McQueen: Margo Mensing
Mississippi: Robert Sulnick
Moulthrop, E: Paul Beswick
Moulthrop, M: Joel Whisenant
Newport: Courtesy of the artist
Niehues: Courtesy of the artist
Nilsson: Hlif Ösp Thorisdottir
Nordenskiöld: Ulla Montan
Parker: Guy Michael Davis
Pliessnig: Courtesy of the artist

Ricourt: Courtesy of the artist
Rossbach: Paul Smith (Rossbach and Westphal)
Rowe: Courtesy of the artist
Ruhwald: Courtesy of the artist
Schreuders: Courtesy of the artist and Jack
Shainman Gallery, New York
Scott: Courtesy of the Artist
Sekimachi: M. Lee Fatherree
Sormin: Anders Sune Berg
Stichter: Courtesy of the Artist
Sundberg: Peter Held
Takamori: Vicky Takamori
Taylor: Andy Hunter
Telford: Fritz Dent
Tsuchiya: Hiroyuki Takenouchi
Voulkos: ASUAM SHP Archive
Werner: Jeff Newton
Wood: ASUAM SHP Archive
Woodman: Bruno Brucchi

Checklist
Pg. 177: # 14, Søren Nielsen
Pg. 178: # 15, Søren Nielsen; # 29, Courtesy of the
artist
Pg. 181: # 59, Courtesy of the artist; # 60, Tom
Grotta; # 61, Bruce Peterson; # 62, Don Nibert, # 64,
Courtesy of the artist; # 65, Courtesy of the artist; #
66, Taylor Dabney

We Are New Here:
Pg. 190: Courtesy of Nao Matsunaga

# CRAFTING A CONTINUUM TOUR ITINERARY

September 7 – December 7, 2013
Arizona State University Art Museum
Tempe, Arizona

January 30 – April 27, 2014
Bellevue Arts Museum
Bellevue, Washington

May 17 – August 10, 2014
Boise Art Museum
Boise, Idaho

September 13 – December 21, 2014
Ft. Wayne Museum of Art
Ft. Wayne, Indiana

January 30 – April 15, 2015
Nora Eccles Museum of Art, Utah State University
Logan, Utah

May 30 – August 30, 2015
Houston Center for Contemporary Craft
Houston, Texas